YOUR DREAM
A Great Challenge

by Pastor Fred Kasule

SHABAR PUBLICATIONS
www.shabarpublications.com

Most Shabar Publications products are available at special quantity discounts for bulk purchase for sales promotions, fund-raising and educational needs. For details, write Shabar Publications at mayorga1126@gmail.com.

Your Dream A Great Challenge
by Pastor Fred Kasule

Published by Shabar Publications
3833 N. Taylor Rd.
Palmhurst, Texas 78573
www.shabarpublications.com

Table of Contents

Anyone can have a dream,
but not everyone can pursue it to the end.
All dreams are given in raw form;
It's your duty to refine them.
Always choose character over comfort,
service over status.
God will bring the success.

Without a dream, people perish.
Without a dream,
People cast off restraint.
Your dream involves other people,
without a people,
A dream perishes.

Dedication

First, to God, who not only speaks but also reveals, through dreams and visions, His plans for us.

Secondly, to my dear wife, Robina, for standing with me daily as we build the dream God has given us.

Thirdly, to my secretary who has typed and re-typed this booklet. Indeed, this little work needed the mercy of God to accomplish it.

My gratitude to Edith, who has helped to edit this book.

Finally, to the directors of GO! International Foundation, members of Cornerstone Christian Fellowship Churches, all who believe in God-given dreams and have prayed for and supported this work.

Foreword

A very inspiring piece of work that comes in at a time when people no longer cherish dreams or nurture themselves in God-given principles to see their dreams come to pass. I encourage you to go ahead and publish it.

-Pastor Micheal Kyazze
Omega Healing Centre

Introduction

I first wrote this book in 2005, and the 2nd print was in 2007.

Your dream is your only bridge from insignificance to a place of significance before God and men in every area of your life.

Whatever God made was for a reason which includes you. The reason behind your existence is what I have called' your dream' in this book. God's plan for your life must become your dream to pursue with all your life. Regardless of circumstances, God has a divine plan for you and your future.

Your talents, skills, and profession must be built around His dream for you. Your future is not ALL up to God. God's dream for you calls for your involvement.

All the things that man has achieved began in the form of dreams. Think of the book you are holding in your hands. I had a God-given desire to put into writing a few Golden principles that make great people out of ordinary ones. Whatever you admire about anybody began as a dream in their heart and mind.

However, much may wish to be like them; you will only duplicate their victories once you know how they became what they were and are today.

Although everybody will indeed end up somewhere, only some people will propose to end up somewhere good. Those few are those who have a picture of their destiny. Your destination is what I have called 'your dream.'

God has His agenda for you, but you must discover and implement it.

When you leave this world, people will remember you either for the problems you solved or brought to them.

God designs your dream to become a vehicle through which you can solve peoples' problems.

-Pastor Fred Kasule
Go International Foundation
Kampala, Uganda, AFRICA

Chapter 1

Your Dream!

Your dream is a challenge not only to you but also to those around you. A challenge is an invitation or call to play a game, run a race, or fight to see who is better or stronger. Your dream is the race set before you. Without a doubt, you will be opposed. But the dream giver has already designed ways of how you can overcome.

A Great Challenge!

Nations and communities have been shaped and transformed by the dreams and visions of every generation. We would still be in the stone age – uneducated or pagans without the dreamers of old.

Each generation is different, but dreamers in every generation have kept the world going. This is true in social, political, economic, and religious circles. You never know what you can accomplish until you get a dream.

Each generation is different, but dreamers in every generation have kept the world going.

"Where there is no vision, the people perish" (Proverbs 29:18)

"My people are destroyed for lack of knowledge." (Hosea 4:6)

According to the above scriptures, people perish because of two reasons. The causes of perishing families, businesses, churches, and nations are due to the lack of vision, dreams, and knowledge.

Once God is the source of your dream, you already have what it will take to fulfill it: His presence.

With God-given dreams, you can confidently walk into your future even before you physically get there.

Do you feel inadequate to accomplish what God has put in your heart? Do you have a fear of failing, insecurity, and low self-esteem? What if you tried and failed? How do you re-source the dream God has given to you? How do your natural visions and God's dreams relate? Is there a relationship between your night dreams and your daily life?

"While we look not at the things which are seen: for the things which are seen are temporal, but the things which are not seen are eternal." (1 Corinthians 4:18)

As we walk to the dream world, which is invisible to the natural man, there are principles in this book that will help you confidently build your God-given dream.

The increased rate of suicide, drug abuse, moral decay, and divorce can only be explained by hopelessness in people's hearts. Without a dream or vision, hope dies. Without a dream or vision, you will spin the wheels and curse the mud.

Without a Dream or Vision, Hope Dies.

As God's people, we must be wise regarding our dreams. We do not want to pursue false hopes that feed our selfishness, lust, or greed.

We need to pray that God places His dreams in our hearts, dreams which are bigger than ourselves, which we will be willing to die for. No matter what kind of problem you have – relational, marital, financial, spiritual, emotional, or vocational - you can find a solution if you have a revelation from God and are willing to obey. My question is, "Do you know His dream for your life?"

A dream is a picture seen by the mind's eye or the power of imagination, during sleep or in a trance-like state. It is a goal or destiny for your life.

The words vision and dream can sometimes be used interchangeably. They all have to do with the power of seeing or imagining, looking ahead, and grasping the truth that underlies facts.

Vision is the ability to catch a glimpse of what God wants to do through your life when you dedicate yourself to Him. Visions and dreams are the languages used in the spirit world. Whether sleeping or as a mental picture, they are like vehicle indicators showing which direction you are taking or are supposed to take.

"Indeed, God speaks once, or twice, yet no one notices. In a

dream, a vision of the night when sound sleep falls on men while they slumber on their beds." (Job 33:14-16)

Dreams are sealed instructions, so we seldom recognize them as coming from God. Many often throw away the answers they ask for when praying for counsel and guidance.

"But as he was thinking this over, behold, an angel of the Lord appeared to him in a dream, saying, Joseph, a descendant of David, do not be afraid to take Mary (as), your wife, for that which is conceived in her is of (from, out of) the Holy Spirit." (Matthew 1:20 Amplified Version)

God frequently communicated with people in the Bible in many ways, including dreams. Joseph, the husband of Mary, was a dream away from God's will.

Saved from Starvation Because of a Dream.

At the peak of civilization, Egypt faced the challenge of severe famine.

The solution to the coming dilemma would be something other than political or economic. If God had not given Pharaoh the two dreams, imagine what could have happened to Egypt and all the nations around it!

Plenty was coming for seven years but a severe famine for another seven years. It is possible to go from the best kind of life to the worst, but God will always reveal a solution. Searching for an interpretation is as crucial as getting the dream itself.

Many individuals, families, businesses, and nations are today blinded by plenty –unaware of the calamities ahead of them. There are also those devastated by crippling situations, but God has a solution. That is why we all need to hear from God, who knows our future in detail. He will always speak. Let us not ignore Him.

"And behold, there came up out of the river, seven fat and sleek, and handsome cows . . . and seven other cows came up after them undernourished, gaunt and ugly such as I have never seen in the whole of Egypt. And ate up the seven fat cows that had come up first and when they had eaten them up, it could not be detected and known that they had eaten them, for they were still thin as at the beginning ... And I saw in my dream and behold seven ears growing on one stalk, plump and good. And behold, seven other ears, withered and thin, devoured the good ones." (Genesis 41:17-24)

Ridiculous dreams, yet the interpretations were sensible! It was God speaking, and nations were saved from starvation. Thank God for dreams and their correct interpretations. Every time God gave a dream, an action was demanded. Positive actions led to positive results and vice versa.

The dream and its symbols must always be interpreted considering the circumstances of the person it is given to. This means that it can only be understood fully by knowing something about the life of the person it concerns.

Although the above examples concern those who dreamt in their sleep, you do not have to be asleep to get a dream from

God concerning your life. The difference between those who fail in life and those who succeed is in dreams. They all have dreams or God-given assignments.

The latter takes time to get the interpretation of those dreams, act and invest resources in them. Dreams increase productivity, breed confidence, strengthen faith, foster better relationships, give direction, and make people tangible assets for their families, churches, organizations, and nations. Lack of dreams brings fear, shame, bitterness, resentment, ill health, low self-esteem, and lack of purpose.

Be determined to have a dream from God for your life because only then can you become an asset to God's kingdom and to those around you.

The Telling of the Dream and Its Interpretation

Although Israel has a covenant with God to be blessed, enjoy God's protection, and prosper, they had been impoverished for seven years. They sowed but never harvested and built houses but lived in dens and caves. Israel had turned from worshipping and serving God to Idols. Disobedience was the cause of this painful seven years.

Whenever you choose to go against God's word, you will always regret the consequences. Think of how many people today live in caves and dens of sickness, poverty, curses, frustrations, and unforgiveness. Indeed, God is not seated in heaven enjoying such misery among His people.

In every generation, God has always found a man or woman willing to develop a relationship with God.

In this very challenging circumstance, God found Gideon.

"When Gideon arrived, behold, a man was telling a dream to his comrade. And he said, Behold, I dreamed a dream, and behold, a cake of barely bread stumbled into the camp of Midian and to the tent and struck it so that it fell, and turned it upside down so that the tent lay flat. And his comrade replied, This is nothing else but the sword if Gideon son of Joash, a man of Isreal. Into his hand God has given the Midian and the host. When Gideon heard the telling of the dream and its interpretation, he worshipped and returned to the camp of Israel and said, Arise, for the Lord has given into your hand the host of Midian." (Judges 7:13-15 Amplified Version)

While growing up, one of the exciting stories I learned in the Bible was of Gideon, who won a big battle with only 300 soldiers, and to make the fight even more interesting, none of them had a single weapon as far as human beings are concerned.

Gideon did not just show up with 300 men one day and win this battle. He had developed a relationship with God. He talked with God and received instructions from Him, which he followed.

Victory depends on our willingness to hear and obey God's voice. Dreams are a series of thoughts or images that we see when we are asleep or awake. They are universal among all men of all times and can affect us either negatively or positively. Worthwhile dreams must be bigger than our abilities and resources. God will always give us dreams that stretch us. A rubber band is no good until it has been pulled. When the interpretation of a dream has been understood, it will give people directions.

When the interpretation of a dream has been understood, it has given the concerned direction.

I have already mentioned that you do not have to sleep to get a dream. Gideon here is a good example. Look at the excuses he gave when God told him that he was a mighty man of valor. He had a background that many of us can identify with.

"And Gideon said to Him, O sir, if the Lord is with us, why is all this befallen us? And where are all His wondrous works of which our fathers told us, saying Did not the Lord bring us up from Egypt? But now the Lord has forsaken us and given us into the hand of Midian. Gideon said to him, Oh Lord, how can I deliver Israel? Behold, my clan is the poorest in Manasseh, and I am the least in my father's house." (Judges 6:13,15 Amplified Version)

God responded to none of his excuses but only promised to be with him.

This is typical of all of us! We want to depend on what we can boast about. These can be our talents, skills, connections, giftings, tribes, or nationalities. Trusting anything that is not

God has an inbuilt failure. Our confidence must be in God.

Trusting Anything that is Not God Has an Inbuilt Failure.

Gideon was an excellent mobilizer. He was able to get 32,000 soldiers within a short time.

"The Lord said to Gideon, the people who are with you are too many for me to give the Midianities into their hands, lest Israel boast themselves against Me, saying, My own hand has delivered me. So now proclaim in the ears of the men, saying, whoever is fearful, and trembling let him turn back and depart from Mount Gilead, and 22,000 remained." (Judges 7:2-3 Amplified Version)

God reduced Gideon's soldiers from 32,000 to 300. Humanly speaking, his fear was justified.

You could be going through a situation of poor health, your finances decreasing, or your relationships and many other things in your life may be deteriorating! Or perhaps you are bound by fear of failure and defeat. That is not the end of the story. The grace that God bestowed upon Gideon is available for you right now.

Gideon is a picture of grace whenever I think about him. Grace is God's ability to be and do what you cannot be and do. This happened in Gideon's life. He struggled with it.

Gideon heard the telling of the dream and its interpretation which encouraged and strengthened him. Although he was still outnumbered in battle, he fought confidently.

All dreams from God are meant to encourage, inform, or warn us. Once you get a dream, begin behaving like you are already there. Gideon started to worship, although the enemies were still there.

Gideon is a Picture of Grace Whenever One Looks at Him.

Gideon was given a strategy for how to win the war. The practical outworking was left to Gideon by inspiration: giving his 300 men a trumpet and a pitcher with a lamp.

Trust Him for the how-to when God gives you a promise, a prophecy, or a dream.

"For we are fellow workmen (joint promoters, labourers together) with and for God; you are God's Garden and field under cultivation, (you are) God's building." (1 Corinthians 3:9 Amplified Version)

We are God's fellow workers in the building of the dreams He gives us. The success of your dream will not be achieved without your participation.

Chapter 2

Your Life Depends on the Dream!

A dream is a state of mind in which images, thoughts, and impressions pass through a person's (heart) mind, sometimes when asleep.

I see your dream as a prophetic revelation of what you can become, do, and have in your lifetime. It is the guiding and motivating force behind every successful man or woman.

People without this kind of guidance and motivation only gamble with their lives. Such a life has no identity, confidence, stability, fullness, or direction. Without a dream for your life, your future will be controlled by circumstances and other people against your own will.

Three sources of the dreams we get:

(1) God, in whose image we were made, has a definite dream for you.
(2) Satan, who can give you the desire to fight against God's purposes on earth. He will also constantly show you pictures of defeat, disease, division, divorce, and death.
(3) People who can inspire you to do something.

My emphasis in this book is on dreams from God. God did not only design your coming into this world but also your future. Regardless of where you were born and where you are now, God has your future in His hands.

"Before you were born, I set you apart to be a prophet to the nations." (Jeremiah 1:5-9)

Jeremiah was set apart to be a prophet before he was born. Maybe you were not set apart to be a prophet, but you were set apart for a purpose, which is God's plan or dream for you.

"...if there is a prophet among you, I the Lord make myself known to him in a vision; I speak to him in a dream." (Numbers 12:6)

I pray that God gives you a revelation of His dream for your life. Life can lose meaning and be empty regardless of the abundance around us. That is why we need to get a revelation from God. However, more is required to have a dream. You should be able to interpret or receive an interpretation for it.

Many people get meaningful dreams while sleeping and never bother searching for interpretations from God or those with a gift to interpret dreams. Such dreams will never help them because the interpretation is unknown, so action needs to be taken.

"The dream is certain and the interpretation of it is sure." (Daniel 2:45 Amplified Version)

King Nebuchadnezzar almost killed Daniel, Shadrach, Meshach and Abednego, and his sorcerers because of a dream he had forgotten, but he demanded an interpretation. Their lives depended on a dream.

"So the decree went forth that the wise men were to be killed, and (the officers) sought Daniel and his companions to be slain." (Daniel 2:13 Amplified Version)

Glory to God for Daniel and his Hebrews friends who knew not the dream but the source of the dream: their God.

Could it be true that you are facing death in your health, family, finances, or any other circumstances? Are you facing a death decree like Daniel and his friends? How do you see your future and that of those around you? I encourage you to do what Daniel and his friends did. Buy yourself time with God alone or with your inner circle; the secret will be revealed.

"And Daniel went in and desired of the king that he would set a date and give him time, and he would show the king the interpretation. Then Daniel went to his house and made the thing known to Hananiah, Mishael, and Azariah, his companions, so that they would desire and request mercy of the God of heaven concerning this secret, that Daniel and his companions should was revealed to Daniel in a vision of the night, and Daniel blessed the God of heaven." (Daniel 2:16-19 Amplified Version)

In most cases, you will need help managing. You need others to stand with you.

"I should state that, if two of you on earth agree (harmonize together, make a symphony together) about whatever (any-

thing and everything) they may ask, it will come to pass and be done for them by My Father in heaven." (Matthew 18:19 Amplified Version)

Daniel and his friends were saved because God showed the dream and its interpretation.

If your life lacks direction in any area, you cannot go wrong when you return to the source of all dreams – God.

Chapter 3

Testimony!

God called me into the ministry when I was about 17, and I thought He had made a mistake! I was so shy that I could not stand before more than five people.

One day in primary school, I was chosen to represent our class on a speech day by reciting a poem. I knew I had memorized it very well. Standing on that platform was a nightmare. I could only speak the first sentence and felt like my inside crumbled. I looked at the hundreds of eyes staring at me and was paralyzed. My mouth could not move anymore, and my memory went blank. I felt sorry for myself, mainly because I had let down my class. With tears running down my cheeks, I left the platform. That incident, simple as it may seem, left a scar in my memory that almost convinced me I would never achieve anything in life.

You may have encountered incidents that have scarred your life and are convinced you will never manage in that area. This problem in my life continued even after getting born again!

In senior school, I worked in a bar, a lodge that men and women frequented for alcohol and other stuff, and that's where I was staying. My experience in that place, as I worked at night and went to school during the day, was heartbreaking. I used to see young girls sometimes in school uniforms defiled by rich older men who brought them to that place. I knew that was not my life portion, so I decided to walk away from that place. Walking away without shoes, I knew my education and future were over. My employer had promised to buy me shoes and had put them in his office. I was excited to have shoes for the first time, but when I told him I was leaving, I also walked away from my long-awaited dream of having a pair of shoes. I was about 16 years old then.

Life had been challenging in the village where I came from after primary education. I had ten other siblings, and I was right in the middle. We used to make our beds by getting poles from the bush, digging holes in the ground, and making a long tablelike thing. Then we would go into the bush again and get grass that we would put in old sacs to make mattresses. My grandfather knew how to push back clothes, the type that dead bodies are put before they are placed in the grave. No running water and no electricity. The thought of ending up in a similar situation was dreadful.

When I walked to my father's two rooms a distance from the bar the following day, one of my sisters requested me to escort her to someplace, but she did not mention the site. We went to where we found about six people, and a man with a Bible walked into the room and began to preach about God's love and plan for all people. That day, I got a revelation that God knew me and had a plan for my life. I kept going to that place for the next 15 years, grounded in the Word and mentored in ministry. I believe that it does not matter your location and condition, God will always place people along the way to help you, but it's your responsibility to embrace those opportunities.

One day a friend asked me to interpret him into Luganda as he preached in English. I knew I could do it, but I thought, "I don't want to let this brother down before a big congregation." I thought again that doing it from behind a curtain would be okay. Anyway, I tried my best that day, and by God's grace, I made it. I got very encouraging comments from the people and suddenly realized that I could always make it with God's help!

You will only know what you can do once you take the first step of faith. It does not matter what your past looks like. You can still make it with God's help.

You Will Only Know What You Can Do Once You Take the First Step of Faith.

I joined a choir but only felt comfortable because I could hide behind others at the back, yet my tenor voice in those days was one of the best in the entire choir. To make matters worse, my life was not that serious with God. I was okay in church but not outside church. My life at that could be best described as a lukewarm life.

When I got tired of my silent frustrations, I separated myself to fast and pray. I determined not to go back home without hearing a definite word from God about my life. I was on a mountain early in the morning, reading my Bible, singing, and praying. Nothing seemed to be happening until late in the afternoon. Satan did not leave me alone. He told me that what I did was just a waste of time. I felt discouraged but decided to persevere though it was almost getting dark.

My prayer was, "Lord, I beseech you to show me Your glory." (Exodus 33:18)

I thought I had fallen asleep or had a trance. I vividly saw the Lord Jesus Christ on the cross; every part of Him was just blood; He was gasping for breath and was undergoing indescribable pain.

For many years I could not describe what I had seen. The only picture close to what I saw is what I recently saw in the movie, *The Passion of The Christ*, by Mel Gibson. Jesus looked at me, and His eyes were like piercing arrows. My eyes could not look at Him. My face was covered with tears. His look was like a laser beam in my eyes. I quickly put my palms over my eyes, but that did not help. This seemed to last ages! I saw Him struggling to speak to me one word at a time. I felt like I was putting on filthy rags. I wanted to run away, but my legs could not carry me. I looked like a heap of rubbish. As I write, I am reminded of Joshua, the high priest.

"Now Joshua was clothed with filthy garments and was standing before the Angel (of the Lord.)" (Zechariah.3:3 Amplified Version)

Imagine a whole high priest in such a situation! Every one of us is constantly accused by Satan before God. No one can ever be good enough without God. It does not matter what you do for Him; without the cleansing work of Jesus' blood, our righteousness is like filthy rags. When you are not right with God, you know it in your heart. It is empty! Empty hearts offer empty worship and empty prayers to God.

Empty Hearts Offer Empty Worship and Empty Prayers to God

"Now, on the final and most important day of the Feast, Jesus stood, and He cried in a loud voice, if any man is thirsty, let him come to me and drink. He who believes in Me (who cleaves to and trusts in and relies on Me) as the Scripture has said, from his innermost being shall flow (continuously) springs and rivers of living water." (John. 7:37,38 Amplified Version)

According to the above Scripture, the outflow depends on the inflow. We must drink of His Spirit and the word first before we can make meaningful worship and prayers to Him. Although the accuser is there daily, I thank God for Jesus Christ our Eternal Advocate.

Back to the vision – He said very slowly and with much pain: This is my blood that was shed for you. Go and be a witness of this blood, and I will watch over you whenever I send you. I then saw a hand giving me tools like those used by a farmer, tools to use while serving God. Now I look at those tools as spiritual gifts given to me to help extend His Kingdom.

I left that mountain, where I had separated myself to pray, a different person. From that day onwards, I received more confidence and courage. That dream or vision made all the difference in my life. Even when things get tough today, I always fall back on that dream and encourage myself in the Lord.

Dreams from God sometimes seem to die, or we sometimes try to ignore them. But if a dream is from Him, it will never let you go!

Maybe God placed something in your heart some time ago that looks dead now. I pray for God's resurrection power to raise it, or perhaps you are trying to avoid the very call on your life. May God give you the courage and determination to stretch your faith and take the first step of seeking and serving Him.

Chapter 4

GO International Foundation!

Years after that encounter, I got a dream of starting a ministry named "GO International Foundation!"

As a ministry, we have a big dream for this foundation. God is raising a team of men and women with a heart to bring hope to the hopeless, help the helpless, salvation to the lost, healing to the broken-hearted, and food to the hungry.

Our primary objective is to preach the risen savior Jesus Christ where He is not known. Since founding this ministry, I have tried to live by the principles I share in this book. This dream in the making has and is still attracting partners and enemies. God is always on our side, even when the going gets tough. I pray that you will pick your side as you read this book!

God is Always on Our Side, Even When the Going Gets Tough.

Our key verses:

"Go then and make disciples of all nations, baptizing them in the name of the Father and the Son and of the Holy Spirit." (Matthew 28:19 Amplified Version)

"For I was hungry, and you gave me food, I was thirsty, and you gave me something to drink, I was a stranger and you brought me together with yourselves, I was naked and you

clothed me, I was sick and you visited me with help and ministering care, I was in prison and you came to see me." (Matthew 25:35)

"What is the use (profit), my brethren, for anyone to profess to have faith if he has no (good) works (to show for it)? Can faith save (his soul)? If a brother or sister is poorly clad and lacks food each day, and one of you says to him, Goodbye, keep yourself warm and well fed, without giving him the necessities for the body, what good does that do? So, also faith, if it doesn't have works (deeds and actions of obedience to back it up), by itself is destitute of power (inoperative, dead)." (James 2:14-17 Amplified Version)

As visionaries and dreamers, we must know that good works are good, but they cannot earn us heaven if one is washed in the blood of Jesus Christ.

One woman had a dream. She had just been born again. She saw a long queue of people approaching the sky in her dream. At the end of the line, she saw a big gate and a gentleman posing questions to whoever approached the big gate. When she was a couple of people away from the entrance, she overheard the gentleman asking the man ahead of her, "What makes you think you deserve a place in heaven?" The man replied, "I was a good man, I was a scout, I helped the poor, I was a good husband and dad" - the list was endless. The gentleman stretched his left hand, and the man fell into the pit of hell. The dreamer trembled because she had done none of that!

The gentleman asked the next person the same question! The

following person said, "I was a preacher, sang in the choir, built a church"; the list of church-based activities was endless. This person also was led to the pit of hell. Meanwhile, the dreamer did not know what to do! She had not done that either, and now it was her turn!

She had the same question, 'Woman, what makes you think you deserve a place in heaven?" suddenly, an answer came, and she said, "Because of the blood of Jesus Christ, which washed my sins away when I got born again recently!" The gentleman stretched his right hand towards heaven's gates, and the newly born-again lady entered heaven.

Before I proceed any further, can you answer that eternal and pertinent question? If you are not sure, now is the time, before you face eternity, to repent of any sin in your life. Jesus' blood can wash you if you repent of every sin you have done in thought, words, and deeds! Whatever we do must be done out of a pure heart.

"And he spoke to those who stood before Him, saying, take away the filthy garments from him. And He said to (Joshua), Behold, I have caused your iniquity to pass from you, and I will clothe you with rich apparel. Let them put a clean turban on his head and clothe him with garments. And the Angel of the Lord stood by." (Zechariah 3:4,5 Amplified Version)

According to the above Scripture, Joshua was still unclean even though he was a high priest. The amount of good works we do for God or man does not matter unless we have a personal relationship with God; we can still be unclean. God gave a command to change the high priest's clothes. God wants to do the same to you. How is your relationship with Him?

"Come now, and let us reason together, says the Lord, though your sins are like scarlet, they shall be white as snow; though they are red like crimson, they shall be like wool." (Isaiah 1:18 Amplified Version)

"My little children, I write to you these things so that you may not violate God's law and sin. But if anyone should sin, we have an Advocate (One who will intercede for us) with the Father – (it is) Jesus Christ (the all-righteous, upright, just, who conforms to the Father's will in every purpose, thought, and action)" (1 John 2:1 Amplified Version)

The above Scriptures are self-explanatory about what God will do for us if we do our part. Such a relationship with God is the foundation upon which you can build any dream.

God's biggest dream is to see the world reconciled to Him through His Son, Jesus Christ. This will have to begin with you. One soul at a time. Perhaps you think, "I am not good enough to be what God wants me to be." You are not alone!

One of the greatest prophets of old was in a similar situation.

"Woe unto me! For I'm undone and ruined because I'm a man of unclean lips, your sin is completely atoned for and forgiven. Whom shall I send? And who will go for us? Then I said, here am I: send me." (Isaiah 6:5-8)

God is still asking us the same question! "Whom shall I send?" Will you allow God to use you as an asset to His Kingdom and society?

As a ministry, we are answering that call by preaching the Gospel where Christ is not yet known, training leaders in our Bible school, planting churches, providing education and a home for orphans and underprivileged children, and offering medical care for those who cannot afford it, giving a meal to the hungry and clothes to the needy. We have witnessed God's provision along the way.

Such provisions would only have come if we had taken the first step of beginning in a tiny way. God is making us grow one step at a time.

We Have Witnessed God's Provision Along the Way.

Never be afraid of beginning in a small way. The source of the dream will always make it grow.

Chapter 5

Spiritual and Practical Responsibilities!

Every dream will only tell you what can be and not what must be, and plans are born in the context of the dreamer's life.

There is nothing spiritual that is not practical, and there is nothing practical that is not spiritual. Lack of balance will bring frustrations and failure even to those with big dreams.

The spiritual world is the parent of the physical world (Hebrews 11:3).

We must never think that whatever God predestined for us will automatically come to pass without our involvement. The Bible contains at least 361 promises, but they all have conditions attached to them. The following scriptures illustrate this.

"IF you will LISTEN DILIGENTLY to the voice of the Lord your God, being watchful to DO ALL His commandments which I command you this day, the Lord your God will SET YOU HIGH ABOVE all the nations of the earth. And all these blessings shall come upon you and overtake you if you heed the voice of the Lord your God." (Deuteronomy 28:1-2 Amplified Version)

"BRING all the tithes (the whole tenth of your income) into the storehouse, that there may be food in my house, and prove me now by it, says the Lord of hosts, IF I will not open

the windows of heaven for you and pour you a blessing out, that there shall not be room enough to receive it." (Malachi 3:10 Amplified Version)

"GIVE, and (gift) will be GIVEN to you; good measure, pressed down, shaken together, and running over, will they pour into (the pouch formed by) the bosom (of your robe and used as a bag). For with the same measure, you deal out (with the measure you use when you confer benefits on others), it will be measured back to you." (Luke 6:38 Amplified Version)

"IF you live in Me (abide vitally united to Me) and My words remain in you and continue to live in your hearts, ASK whatever you will, and it shall be done for you." (John 15:7)

The above scriptures emphasize our role if we are to enjoy God's blessings in every area of our lives. The success of your dream will not come without your participation.

There is Nothing Spiritual That is Not Practical and Nothing Practical That is Not Spiritual.

While pursuing my degree in Economics and Statistics at the university, I would stay on campus from Monday through Friday. Most weekends, I was somewhere preaching. Towards examination time, two of my friends, a Muslim and a Catholic, ridiculed and laughed at me. I felt embarrassed. They told me that I would fail my examinations because I was not reading and revising as hard as they thought I should. What they were doing and saying was discouraging me from ministry.

The Success of Your Dream Will Not Be Without Your Participation.

One night I had a dream. I saw an animal running after me and these two friends. I outran it. Looking back, I noticed that the animal had caught my catholic friend, but he escaped and outran it too. I looked again and saw that this animal had caught and overcome my Muslim friend. The next day I narrated this dream to my two friends. I did not know what it meant, but my Catholic friend immediately interpreted it. He said the 'animal' was none other but the exams. "It seems Fred will pass with flying colors; I will fail some papers, but it doesn't look good for our Muslim friend." I was encouraged and unafraid when I entered the main hall to sit for these exams. I knew God was with me. I knew the weekends I had spent serving God were not in vain. The results were as the dream had portrayed for the three of us.

"You have said, it is useless to serve God, and what profit is it if we keep His ordinance and walk gloomy and as if in mourning apparel before the Lord of hosts?" (Malachi 3: 14 Amplified Version)

According to the above scripture, serving God with our time, talents, and treasures is not useless. The consequences are eternal when we choose to serve or not serve God.

Never be too busy to serve God because you are building your dream. Time spent serving God is never wasted. It is only invested. And He knows how to make us profitable.

Time Spent Serving God is Never Wasted. It Is Only Invested.

God desires that all get saved and go to heaven, but no – one will get saved without their participation.

"Because you acknowledge and confess with your lips that Jesus is Lord and, in your heart, believe (adhere to, trust in, and rely on the truth) that God raised him from the dead, you will be saved." (Romans 10:8,9 Amplified Version)

The above scripture shows that your part is to acknowledge that you are a sinner. The next step is to speak with your mouth what you have believed in your heart.

God delights in the prosperity of His servants, but no one will prosper when they do not respond to His word.

"HONOUR the Lord with your wealth, with the first fruit of all your crops; THEN your barns will be filled to overflowing and your vats will brim over with new wine." (Proverbs 3:9,10)

God's plan to prosper you includes working, giving, and managing your possessions God's way.

According to the above Scripture, you cannot just pray and wait for your barns to overflow until you honor the Lord with your wealth.

The above text shows that what you do with your treasure will determine the measure of God's blessing upon your dream.

Victory awaits every dreamer if willing to act on God's promise and direction. God cannot be the source of your success when He is not the source of your standard. Many are still stuck even after hearing from God because they are too lazy to act.

Remember Hannah when Eli spoke a blessing to her?

"Then Eli answered and said, go in peace: and the God of Israel grant you your petition that you have asked of Him."

"The family rose early in the morning, worshipped before the Lord, and returned to their home in Ramah, Elkanah knew his wife, and the Lord remembered her." (1 Samuel 1:19 Amplified Version)

Hannah had a problem of barrenness, and for years she was tormented by her rival who had children. Her dream was to bear a male child. The passion for a male child could not allow her to eat. She was heartbroken at home, and even when she went to church, her pastor mistook her for being drunk. But she did not resent her pastor. Instead, she explained her situation and was finally encouraged by the high priest. After hearing from the man of God, she returned sad no more.

But that was not the end of the story. She had to fulfill her marital obligation to her husband, but this time with a divine blessing, her dream of a male child was fulfilled. It's possible to do the right things and still fail. But with divine empowerment, you will always win regardless of past failures.

Nothing of Value Happens Overnight.

Prayer alone is not enough if you do not listen to God speak into your situation through the word, the Holy Spirit, a dream, a vision, His servants, or circumstances, and obeying the instructions. I pray that God opens your spiritual ears today so that you hear God speak words of encouragement and victory. Whatever He says, DO it.

Whenever God gives you a dream, His strategic provisions will come along the way. When you do not know what to do and how to do it, you must call upon Him.

"Call to Me and I will answer you and show you great and mighty things, fenced in and hidden, which you do not know (do not distinguish and recognize, have the knowledge and understand.)" (Jeremiah 33:3 Amplified Version)

The above scripture gives you access to His throne. Sometimes the things we need to progress in our dreams seem fenced and hidden. The key to hidden treasures is prayer. Let God be your best partner once His will is revealed to you. Do what you can, and let God do the rest.

The people whose dreams you admire have behind their stories of adversity, suffering, fears, name it. Building a dream that will last takes time. Nothing of value happens overnight!

Chapter 6

Sowing and Reaping!

As you pursue, help others achieve theirs too. The truth is that the more people you help to achieve their dreams, the quicker you will achieve yours.

Sometime back, a lady hosted us for a wonderful lunch. During the conversation, I asked her how long she had lived in her neighborhood. "Pastor, I have lived here and have been building this house for the last 30 years, and it is not yet finished." To me, it was a mansion!

My second question was, "Why?" She confessed she had six children, and her husband had to care for them while growing up. They needed education, and whoever reached 18 would need a car, and it was their responsibility to help each of them.

This couple helped all their children achieve their dreams. These children will want to help their parents complete their dream house. You can't fail to succeed when you make others successful.

"There are those who (generously) scatter abroad, and yet increase more; there are those who withhold more than is fitting or what is justly due, but it results only in want. The liberal person shall be enriched, and he who waters shall himself be watered. The people curse him who holds back grain (when the public needs it), but a blessing (from God

and man) is upon the head of him who sells it." (Proverbs 11:24-26)

A striking statement on the cover of Bill Clinton's book My life reads his career (dream) was shaped by his resolute determination to improve the lives (other people's dreams) of his fellow citizens.

Bill Clinton writes, I always tried to keep things moving in the right direction, to give more people a chance to live their dreams, to lighten people's spirits, and to bring them together. That is the way I kept the score. I like the attitude this man had and hopefully still has. It is worth taking on board. We must help others in the process of achieving their God-given dreams.

To Succeed, You Must Learn to Serve.

"For even the son of man came not to have service rendered to Him, but to serve, and to give His life as a ransom for (instead of) many." (Mark 10:45 Amplified Version)

The above Scripture shows the heart of our Lord Jesus Christ. Although He was and is the Son of God, Creator of all human beings, He became a servant to humanity. To be successful, we must follow in His footsteps.

The mercy we sow into others is not because they deserve it but because we will deserve it later.

Joseph served his brothers, Potiphar, fellow prisoners, and

the pharaoh. No wonder he prospered wherever he served. (Genesis 37 and 41.)

Please take some time to read those chapters. They have eternal truths that will help anybody with a dream.

Dreamers sow into others what they will need others to sow into them. There is a saying, 'The mercy we sow into others is not because they deserve it but because we will deserve it later.'

I have always had a desire to have a media ministry. One day a brother hosted us on his radio program. After the program, I asked him what his needs were. He had a huge debt for his program. I sowed a seed telling God I am believing You for a media ministry. Today, I minister on several radio stations and television. I have been in different programs locally and internationally. The seed I sowed then opened and is still opening media doors.

Chapter 7

The Success of Your Dream Depends On Its Source and Those Around You.

There are two types of dreams: those birthed by the flesh and those birthed by the Spirit.

"What is born of (from) the flesh (of the physical is physical); and what is born of the spirit is of the Spirit." (John 3:6 Amplified Version)

Dreams born out of the flesh are of no eternal value. They only portray selfishness, greed, and pride. You will be surprised by the number of people tormented by dreams God never gave them.

If the source is not God, He has not equipped you for it. Everybody ends up somewhere: and very few end up somewhere on purpose; these are the ones with dreams from God.

When you are sure that the source of your dream is God, along with the courage to see it through, it dramatically increases your chances of reaching the end of your life, looking back with satisfaction that you succeeded and finished well. You must involve God in whatever you do.

"For I am already about to be sacrificed (my life is about to be poured out as a drink offering); ... I have fought the good (worthy, honorable, and noble) fight, I have finished the race, I have kept (firmly held) the faith. (As to what

remains) henceforth there is laid up for me the (victor's) crown of righteousness (for being right with God and doing right), which the Lord, the righteous judge, will award to me only, but also to all those who have loved and yarned for and welcomed His appearing (His return)." (2 Timothy 4:6-8 Amplified Version)

You can confidently say with Paul the Apostle, "My life counted; I made a difference." Make your place a better place than when you found it. This could be a home, business, church, school, political party, or nation.

Make the Place Where You Are a Better Place Than When You Found It.

Who is the source of your dream?

Before we proceed, let me state once again what a dream is. It is a creative idea from God, revealed to man's mind. For the dream to be effective, it must come from God. This God-given dream determines everything in the process of a successful life. We all have a natural desire to become somebody. For example, a doctor, a lawyer, a preacher, a businessperson, a policeman, a pilot, etc.

We also desire to possess big things, but why do we want all that? Whatever we believe in should be for God's glory and must be a tool to serve God with.

In answering this question, search yourself! Who are you trying to impress? Are your efforts for achievement trying to prove to someone that you can make it without them? Earthly achievements without God are always contaminated with selfishness.

They breed a need to control others, a need for recognition, and a need to exploit others. Believe me; this has an inbuilt element of failure.

If the dream is from God, no matter how long it takes, wait for God's timing, prepare yourself thoroughly, and go only when he says, "GO."

Unless God is the source of your dream, business, marriage, and ministry, the question of life's purpose becomes meaningless.

The purpose of life can be a puzzle when you begin from the wrong point. Many ask themselves questions like, "What do I want to be?", "What should I do with my life?", "What are my goals for the future?"

It Is a Creative Idea from God, Revealed to the Mind of Man for Him to Carryout.

We must all remember that God is not just a starting point of our lives but is its actual source.

"For it was in Him that all things were created, in heaven and on earth, things seen and things unseen, whether thrones, dominions, rulers or Authorities; all things were created and exist through him (by his service, intervention)

and in and for him". (Colossians 1:16 Amplified Version)

"In His hand is the life of every living and the breath of all mankind." (Job. 12:10 Amplified Version)

Most people know the story of Job. He was once a wealthy man, but he lost everything momentarily. But because he trusted God, whatever he lost was restored two times. Life is about letting God use you for his purpose rather than using Him for your purposes.

"For we are his workmanship, created in Jesus Christ for good works that we shall work in them." (Ephesians 2:10)

Life is About Letting God Use You for His Purposes Rather Than You Use Him for Your Purposes.

The word WORKMANSHIP means 'to make.' It signifies that which is manufactured, a product. It means a design produced by an artisan. Design dictates purpose. For instance, my van is designed to carry seven passengers. Other vans can carry up to 14 passengers.

Carrying 14 passengers in my van would be an overload, and my dear van would break down quickly. God's purpose for me is different from yours. That is why he has endowed us with other talents and skills. Those who have not discovered God's dreams for their lives are overloaded with care, and their deaths, PHYSICAL OR SPIRITUAL, are just around the corner.

GOOD WORKS mean righteousness, health, and wealth.

"The generation of the upright shall be blessed. Prosperity and welfare are in his house and his righteousness endures forever." (Psalm 112:2b-3 Amplified Version)

Our designer prepared beforehand that we should walk in prosperity and welfare. We all have a share in these good works.

If You Want to Do More, You Must Become More.

Suppose you want to fly from one place to another. Your responsibility as a passenger is to have your ticket and get onto the plane. The way to your destination is the pilot's concern. He knows how to get there. You don't jump off the aircraft when you encounter any turbulences or air pockets! You make sure your seat belt is on and follow the instruction.

Only God knows the way to your future. Your responsibility is to follow His instructions even when things are bumpy. Let Him be the pilot of every area of your life.

"Only you be strong and courageous, that you may do according to all the laws which Moses my servant commanded you, turn not from it to the right hand or to the left, that you may prosper wherever you go." (Joshua 1:7 Amplified Version)

After the death of Moses, God's dream for Israel had to continue. He chose Joshua, whom Moses had mentored to continue. The good thing is that Joshua learned to hear from God, which is how he could prosper.

Such a revelation cannot be unless there is a relationship with God.

"And Jesus said to them, come after me and be my disciples, and I will make you become fishers of men." (Mark. 1:17 Amplified Version)

Jesus Christ (not time, talent, or treasure) has the power to make you become before you can perform. He had to mold his disciples before sending them out. The saying is true if you want to do more, you must become more.

Chapter 8

Pre-Planned Life!

If it is true that God knew us and planned our lives even before birth, how come one person moves forward with one success after another while some are still getting ready? How come one man goes through life overcoming one problem after another while another goes from defeat to defeat, struggling and getting nowhere?

A man made a living by selling balloons at a fair. He had all sorts of colored balloons. Whenever business was slow, he would release a helium-filled balloon into the air, and kids would come and buy his balloons. One day, he felt someone tugging at his jacket. Turning around, he saw a little boy who asked, "If you release a black balloon, would it also fly?"

Moved by the boy's concern, the man replied, "Son, it is not the color of the balloon; it is what is inside that makes it go up."

This is what happens even in our lives. It is what is on the inside which counts. It is not the race, country, or tribe we belong to; if we have God's dreams, we will reach our destination.

The two pillars that will make your lifeline up to God's dream for you are Decisions and Discipline. For every dream, there must be goal setting and goal getting. The future of your dream is shaped by the type of decisions you make and how you implement and manage these decisions daily. Every dream must have a starting point; otherwise, it will be like any other wish. Many people have targets for their lives but never take the courage to pull the trigger-they start.

When I decided to marry my sweetheart, it was not a one-time decision, and I waited for the wedding day. I knew I would not wake up someday before a pastor in a church, go to the reception hall, and then to the honeymoon without my involvement from the first decision time. It took me a whole year to work daily on our relationship. It was a daily discipline up to the wedding day. The discipline and decisions continue daily!

Notre Dame admonished, "You don't make decisions because they are easy, cheap, or popular. You make decisions because they are right."

Every Dream Must be Committed to Paper.

"And the lord answered me and said, write the vision and engrave it so plainly upon tablets that everyone who passes may (be able to) read (it easily and quickly) as he hastens by. For the vision is yet for an appointed time and it hastens to the end (fulfillment); it will not deceive or disappoint. Though it tarry, wait (earnestly) for it, because it will surely come; it will not be behindhand on its appointed day." (Habakkuk 2:2-4 Amplified Version)

The above scripture encourages us to write whatever God puts on our hearts. Can you imagine what would have happened if God had spoken and no one accepted the responsibility of writing the scriptures?

We would have no instructions to follow, and our lives would be unmanageable. Can you imagine a stranger in a big city without a journey planner? That is how life would be without God's word.

It is said that "dilute ink is more powerful than your brains." It is easy to forget something, but once you commit it onto paper, chances are that whoever reads your dream-if it is to build God's kingdom or help fellow human beings will want to play a part in it. Men have a desire to be part of a noble cause. Your dream, committed on paper, will continue even after you are gone. What would you do if someone came to your office and asked for a contribution for a wedding, but they had no budget? My first advice would be to make a budget before proceeding; make a decision today and discipline yourself to put every dream that God will reveal to you on paper.

Every Good Dream Needs Good Decisions.

John Maxwell says, *decisions help us start; discipline helps us finish.*

We are all creatures of comfort and want to avoid pain at all costs. Discipline, in whatever area of your life, will be painful.

Sometimes we only wish to pursue things that have proven effective in the past. However, if we want to go beyond past dreamers, we must be willing to try new ventures.

All Bible champions made decisions that affected their lives tremendously, but the rewards are eternal.

In Genesis 12, Abraham obeyed God and left his home country for a land he did not know. I am sure he trusted that whatever God had for him was good though he had not seen it yet. When God speaks, you must trust and obey Him.

Failure to Endure the pain of discipline means ever living with the pain of regret.

Moses took courage and forsook earthly treasures to carry out God's dream for his life. Millions of people were and are still blessed because of his decision (Heb.11:24-27).

"And Ruth said, urge me not to leave you or to turn back from following you; for where you go, I will go, and where you lodge, I will lodge. Your people will be my people and your God my God. Where you die, I will die, and there will I be buried. The Lord do so to me, and more also, if anything but death parts me from you." (Ruth. 1:16,17: Amplified Version)

Ruth was a gentile widow, but God rewarded her for leaving her country and following her mother-in-law. She got married to a wealthy man and also shared the lineage of our savior.

"Salmon the father of Boaz, whose mother was Rahab, Boaz the father of Obed, whose mother was Ruth, Obed the fa-

ther of Jesse." (Matthew 1:5 Amplified Version)

Your God-given dream may dictate that you move from one location to another. Through their decisions and the rewards they got on earth, not to mention the eternal heavenly rewards, I am sure Ruth's family had to be well disciplined to endure the challenges. Failure to endure the pain of discipline means ever living with the pain of regret.

We live in an imperfect world with imperfect people who sometimes influence us to make wrong decisions. The Dream Giver knows you will get it wrong sometimes, but you should not build a monument at your place of failure.

A righteous man shall fall seven times, but the Lord promises to raise him again. What if you had been Jonah? Would you have kept silent in the fish's belly? Read Jonah 2. Maybe you have made many mistakes before, but if you are reading this book, I can assure you that you are not a mistake yourself. Wrong choices can vomit you up now if you call on the Lord and ask for wisdom for better choices.

"And the Lord spoke to the fish, and it vomited out Jonah upon the dry land." (Jonah 2:10 Amplified Version)

People Don't Drown by Falling in the Water But by Staying in the Water.

Whoever lacks wisdom should pray for it. However, you need to learn from the past and move on.

The saying is true that people do not drown by falling in the water but by staying in the water,

How Are You Handling Your 3 "Ts?"

Whatever God has given you: time, talents, and treasure must be used in your generation and line with God's will.

"For David after he had served God's will and purpose and counsel in his own generation, fell asleep (in death) and was buried among his forefather, and he did see corruption and undergo putrefaction and dissolution (of the grave)." (Acts.13:36 Amplified Version)

David risked his life by using his faith and courage to deliver Israel from Goliath. He used his musical talents to relieve King Saul whenever an evil spirit tormented him. He used his shepherd's heart to rule over Israel. He used his wealth to prepare for the building of the temple. Although he did not do it, his son Solomon implemented this dream for the Temple. After all this and much more, he slept!

You cannot just take your talents, experiences, opportunities, and education and run off in any direction you please.

God loves us all equally, but if it is true that our lives were pre-planned before birth, why do many live regrettable lives? You see, there are two types of pain: the pain of regret and the pain of discipline.

We are not robots. The quality of your decisions will shape

the destiny of God's dream for you.

Never Be a Prisoner of Your Past!

Recently, one of our newspapers reported and showed pictures of a lady who had left the home of a very wealthy man with a big, storied house. She had gone back to selling passion fruit juice in the market. When asked why she said, "I am more peaceful here than there." That speaks volumes!

Sometimes the people we admire are not that satisfied. Satisfaction comes only when we are what God wants us to be and doing what He wants us to do where He wants us to do it.

A story is told of a couple who had two boys. The father was an alcoholic and was very violent toward his wife and their sons. He was physically and verbally abusive to them. When the boys grew up, one decided to be like his father. He married and had children but became physically and verbally abusive. His younger brother was also married and had children. He had a wonderful family; he educated his children and was successful. It wasn't easy to believe they had grown up in the same family. One inquisitive person visited both their homes. He asked the young man who was abusive to his family why he behaved the way he did. The young man told him, "I grew up seeing my dad behave this way, so I decided to behave like him. "To him, abuse and violence at home was normal. The inquirer left and visited the other brother, who was doing well. The question was posed, "Why are you different from your brother" The young man replied, "I grew up in a family where my father was very abusive to our mom and us, but I decided that when I grow up, I will not behave like my dad." They had grown up in the same environment but lived differently. The story demonstrates the power of choice.

Never allow your lousy past to shape your future. May God help you make the right decisions in your circumstances today! Never be a prisoner of your past!

Our lives are like concrete. The shape of concrete depends on the cast in which it is poured. The container which shapes our lives and destiny is our decision-making. Some people who come to you for counsel are not seeking counsel. Some have already decided about an issue but are looking for someone to support them and blame them if things go wrong!

We must, therefore, only advise and not make decisions for others.

Chapter 9

Speculation or Revelation?

Speculation is concluding something without having complete knowledge of it. It is guesswork. The risk of loss and failure is very high. People who gamble with their lives are a risk to society. It would be best if you lived by revelation. Revelation is when a hidden secret is made plain.

"For I know the thoughts and plans that I have for you, says the Lord, thoughts, and plans for welfare and peace and not for evil, to give you hope in your final outcome." (Jeremiah 29:11 Amplified Version)

The above Scripture assures us of God's thoughts and concern for us. God's dream for your life can only be achieved by revelation. Revelation can come as a dream, a vision, an impression, a knowing, or another way. It is basically the "What did you see, hear or receive from God"? However, all this would be useless without an interpretation.

"What do you see?" (Jeremiah 1:11)

The verse above gives an interpretation of what the prophet had seen.

The interpretation is the "What is God saying"? Or "What does this mean"? When you get a revelation, it will call for application once the meaning has been made known. Application is understanding how we implement or utilize the revelation and interpretation we receive. It is the "What do I do with this dream?" You did not create yourself, so there is no way you can tell yourself what to do. It is your responsibility to seek God's plan for your every situation.

A proud dad of an 18-year-old boy walked into the room where we were. He told everybody in the room, you know what? My son turned 18 and has just asked for a toy! I could not figure out how an 18-year-old would fancy a doll for a birthday present. Soon after, the boy entered our room with two barrels of a brand-new big hunting gun. I do not remember holding a gun before, but he handed it to me. I beheld the glory of his turning 18. Anyway, I confessed to him that I had never held a gun before, which meant I had never pulled a trigger. Looking closely at the place near the trigger, these words were engraved: "Do not use before reading the manual." Suddenly, I felt I could use it for hunting if only I could get my hands on the manual, the how-to book.

Do Not Use Before Reading the Manual.

God's word is the 'How-To' Book for your lifetime. It is necessary to seek Him, study His word, and have goals or dreams for your life. One must never be too busy focusing on goals and dreams or even taking steps towards implementing your heart's desires before talking to God first. Should I wait for God to tell me whether to be a lawyer, a doctor, etc., before I proceed? I believe God can put a desire in your heart to pursue a profession.

"Delight yourself also in the Lord, and He will give you the

desires and secret petitions of your heart." (Psalm 37:4: Amplified Version)

That desire should become your dream to pursue. However, that dream should never contradict the values of God's word but must be used for God's glory.

Suppose a student makes a wrong decision by sleeping with a man and getting pregnant. She may have the desire to continue with her education without having to care for the child. Deciding to abort a child would be wrong, although the desire to continue with her academics would be right. Any desire or decision contradicting the written Word is wrong and has negative consequences.

Although God wants you to prosper, you must not choose to lie or take a bribe to achieve this. Although He wants you to have favor, you must not lower your values by selling your body or discrediting others to gain favor.

All That God Desires for You Must Be Achieved in God's Way.

I have listened to hundreds of heartbroken lives, and most of the time, the cause has been operating outside God's will or giving up too soon on what they know they should be doing.

We must not be impatient with God. We need child-like faith to trust God, who knows what He is doing with us. God calls you to seek counsel from His word and Godly people.

"Where no wise guidance is, the people fall, but in the multitude of counselors there is safety." (Proverbs 11:14 Amplified Version)

"WHOEVER LOVES instruction and correction loves knowledge, but he who hates reproof is like a brute beast, stupid and indiscriminating." (Proverbs 12:1 Amplified Version)

"Whoever despises the word and counsel (of God) brings destruction upon himself, but he who (reverently) fears and respects the commandment (of God) is rewarded." (Proverbs 13:13 Amplified Version)

"Where there is no counsel, purposes are frustrated, but with many counselors, they are accomplished." (Proverbs 15:22: Amplified Version)

Life is very short. We must abide by God's grace and try to gain the most out of every moment of life and move to the next big challenge.

A person named Once Bill said that even when I wasn't sure where I was going or what I was doing, I was always in a hurry.

Is that true of your life? Why hurry when you need to figure out where you are going? Many have rushed into relationships, businesses, and ministries, regretting it later.

We need the Holy Spirit to help us in all that we do. Without

Him, silent frustrations will be the result. His work is to teach us all things.

"But the comforter (counselor, helper, intercessor, advocate, strengthener, standby), the Holy Spirit, whom the Father will send in my name (in my place, to represent me and act on my behalf) He will teach you all things. "And He will cause you to recall (will remind you of, bring to your remembrance) everything I have told you." (John 14:26)

Chapter 10

Who Holds the Key to the Future of Your Dream?

Most people are anxious about what their tomorrow holds. They will travel distances, spend and be willing to be spent if they can get to know their future.

One day, as I was walking on a street in east London, somebody came from behind and suddenly offered me his hand as a greeting. Although I did not know this person, I innocently responded by shaking his hand. He could not let my hand go, and immediately he looked at the palm of my hand and began to tell me how bright my future was, etc. I immediately recognized that he was a palm reader and raised my voice and said that what he told me was nothing new. I knew it all. He asked me how I knew it, and I retorted, "I have Jesus, the source of all knowledge, He is my Savior and Friend, and He has good plans for you." The gentleman let go of my hand and slipped away. Many people have fallen victim to such people because they tell them what they want to hear or intimidate them with prophecies of doom.

"For I know the thoughts and plans that I have for you, says the Lord, thoughts, and plans for welfare and peace and not for evil, to give you hope in your final outcome." (Jeremiah 29:11 Amplified Version)

You are not a stranger to God. Your path is already paved; you only need to agree with him. Let Him lead the way.

"These are the words of the Holy one, the true one, He who has the key of David, who opens, and no one shall shut, who shuts and no one shall open." (Revelation 3:7 Amplified Version)

God holds the key to your future, not others. It is only Him who can influence others on your behalf. Do not try to manipulate certain people thinking they will open the right door for you or that they are your dream's source and resource, only to become resentful when it does not happen.

If God is the source of your dream, He will also resource it. Your responsibility is to approach His throne, and He, in turn, will approach peoples' hearts on your behalf.

You Already Have What It Takes to Begin On Your Dream.

Stop saying I do not have what it takes to do what God has told me to do! God has provided you with everything you need to start the journey to where you should be. Whatever you do not have now will come along the way.

"...But make me a little cake of (it) first and bring it to me." (1 Kings 17:13b Amplified Version)

"For thus says the Lord, the God of Israel: The jar of meal shall not waste away or the bottle of oil fail until the day that the Lord sends rain on the earth." (vs. 14 Amplified Version)

A widow and her son were just a meal away from death. Elijah was their deliverer. Although he did not come with bags of rice and oil tins, he came with God's word. God had also spoken to the widow before Elijah came.

"...Behold, I have commanded a widow there to provide for you." (vs. 9b Amplified Version)

Obedience to God's word saved her household. God will never ask from you what he has not first given you. The little talent, time, and treasure you have put in His hands will always be multiplied. Nothing in God's hands shrinks. If it does, it is because he wants to multiply it. Someone is your Elijah, your deliverer, although he may look needy. Walk in obedience if you want God to sustain you in your season of famine.

The rod Moses used to rear his father-in-law's sheep became God's supernatural weapon against Pharaoh and the whole of Egypt.

"And the lord said to him, what is that in your hand? And he said, A rod." (Exodus 4:2)

A boy had five loaves of bread and two fishes which Jesus multiplied to feed thousands of people. Read Mark 6:38.

When you ask the Lord to show you what you should begin with, He will, and it will always be within your reach.

A story is told of a wise man who came to talk to a poor farmer about the glory of diamonds. The wise man said, "If you had a diamond the size of your head, you could own a city." That night the farmer could not sleep; he became unhappy and discontented. The following morning, he made arrangements and sold off his farm, cared for his family, and went in search of the diamond. He searched everywhere but could not find any diamonds. He reached Spain when he was emotionally, physically, and financially broken. He threw himself into the river Barcelona and drowned. Back home, the person who had bought his farm fed camels at a stream that ran through the farm when he noticed sunrays hit a stone, making it sparkle like a rainbow. Drawing nearer, he picked up the stone and put it in the living room of his house. That afternoon, the wise man visited him. He noticed the stone and said to the man, "That is a diamond." The new farm owner replied, "No, it's just a stone I picked from the stream." He took the wise man to the stream from where he had picked the stone. To their dismay, they discovered the farm was indeed covered with acres of diamond.

You Are an Answer to Someone's Prayer - Will you be obedient?

In the same way, if you have God within you, you are walking on acres of wealth. Many times, the opportunity is under our feet. We may not have to go anywhere to look for it. The grass on the other side may look greener, but if God is not there, stay where you are. Others are eyeing the grass on our side as we eye the other side. People without a dream will always complain of noise when opportunity knocks. Remember, the same opportunity never knocks twice. The next opportunity may be far better or worse.

I pray that God opens your eyes to see the treasure within and without you. May you discover and develop it to serve your generation.

"For l always pray to the God of our Lord Jesus Christ, that He may grant you a spirit of wisdom and revelation in the knowledge of Him, by having the eyes of your heart flooded with light." (Ephesians 1: 17)

All you must do is walk in obedience to God's word. We all have untapped potential in many areas. Instead of envying others' success, let us concentrate on developing what God has endowed us with. It is not who has the most who wins, but the one who knows how to use whatever they have.

"I returned and saw under the sun that the race is not to the swift nor the battle to the strong, neither is bread to the wise nor riches to men of intelligence and understanding nor favor to men of skills, but time and chance happens to them all." (Ecclesiastes 9:11)

Dick Biggs said, *the greatest gap in life is between knowing and doing.*

Stop complaining about what you do not have and use what you already have.

"(Not in your own strength) for it is God who is all the while effectually at work in you (energizing and creating in you the power and desire), both to will and to work for His good pleasure and satisfaction and delight" (Philippians 2:13 Amplified Version)

Gods power is available for you. He is not looking for your abilities. He is willing to work with whoever is available. God has the master key for every door of your life, but he usually uses someone to open it for you.

God used Moses to deliver Israel.

God used Mordecai to take care of Esther, who was an orphan. He was also used to prevent the king from being assassinated; God used Esther to deliver the Hebrews from the wrath of Haman.

You also hold the key to someone's dream somewhere. It does not matter where you are, what you have, or what you do not have; people who need you are all around you. May God open your eyes to see where you can sow your time, talent, and treasure. You are an answer to someone's prayer; will you be obedient?

Chapter 11

Your Dream Is a Magnet!

A magnet is a piece of metal that can attract metal. Your God-given dream can attract different categories of people into your life.

A young Scots boy, Andrew Carnegie, went to America and started doing odd jobs. He had a dream of becoming wealthy and was willing to pursue it. He ended up as one of the largest steel manufacturers in the United States of America. At one time, 43 millionaires were working for him.

Someone once asked him how he dealt with people. He replied that dealing with people is like digging for gold; when digging for an ounce of gold, you must move tons of dirt. But when digging, you do not look for the dirt; you are looking for gold.

You will find it if you look for what is wrong with people. But every person that will come your way has something positive in them. Someone once said that even a stopped clock is right twice a day. You don't want people like a stopped clocked to be involved in your dreams. People will want to distract, delay, discourage, overtake, or even destroy your dream.

Think about David.

"And when the Philistines heard that David was anointed king over all Israel, (THEY) all went up to seek David. And

(he) Heard of it and went out before them." (1 Chronicles 14:8 Amplified Version)

When the Philistines heard that David had been anointed king over all of Israel, they all went to search for him. The rest of the story shows that they were not looking for him to congratulate him. Certainly not even to encourage him in his new assignment.

Notice they heard that he had been anointed. Look at your assignment as your God-given dream. Something you have been called or equipped for will make the enemy want to attack and destroy you.

Whenever you face a storm, do what David did. Although he was a king and had troops, he knew where to go first. He prayed to God, and he was given instructions. No wonder he said, "God has broken through my enemies."

Instructions from your dream's source will always precede a breakthrough in your dreams. Are you facing an attack on your health, marriage, family, business, or ministry? You are just a prayer away from your breakthrough.

"And the Philistines again made a raid in the valley..." (vs. 13 Amplified Version)

Instructions from the Source of Your Dream Will Always precede a Breakthrough in Your Dream.

Past victories in your dream do not mean you will not be attacked again. David did not depend on his past method of winning the battle. He was given different instructions when he inquired of the Lord again.

"And David inquired again of God, and God said to him, do not go up after them; turn away from them and come (around) upon them over opposite the mulberry trees. And when you hear a sound of marching the tops of the mulberry or balsam trees, then go out to battle, for God has gone out before you to smite the Philistine host." (vs. 14-15 Amplified Version)

It took obedience and patience on the part of David to defeat the Philistines. People of dreams do not depend on past proven methods but on current instructions from God. Your next breakthrough is an instruction away from God. What is God saying about your circumstance? You may need a moment right now to inquire of the Lord! Why not do it now? Take a moment to talk to Him now!

Let us look at Mordecai.

"But he scorned laying hands only on Mordecai. So, since they had told him Mordecai's nationality, Haman sought to destroy all the Jews, the people of Mordecai throughout the whole kingdom of Ahasuerus." (Esther 6:10 Amplified Version)

Mordecai was a Jew in captivity. He refused to bow to Haman, who was second in command to the king. Haman made plans to destroy all the Jews but particularly Mordecai. However,

God's plan for Mordecai was to replace Haman.

"The king said to Haman, make haste and take the apparel and the horse, as you have said, and do so to Mordecai the Jew, who sits at the king's gate. Leave out nothing that you have spoken." (Esther 6: 10: Amplified Version)

Haman was destroyed after the Jews had prayed and fasted.

Notice that before Mordechai's promotion, Haman sought to kill him. In many cases, tragedies always come before testimonies. If you are facing one now, trust and pray to God. Exaltation is your portion in Jesus' name!

Joseph had to deal with Potiphar's wife every day. Such attacks and temptations will come your way just before your promotion. Never give in because this will destroy your dream.

"...she spoke to Joseph day after day, but he did not listen to her, to lie with her or to be with her." (Genesis 39:10 Amplified Version)

No matter how robust your dream is, one wrong relationship can ruin a plan built for years.

Welcoming a Jonah in your boat means embracing a storm.

"But the Lord sent out a great wind upon the sea, and there was a violent tempest in the sea so that the ship was about to be broken." (Jonah 1:3-4 Amplified Version)

Disobedient Jonah caused the sailors to lose their cargo, and they almost lost their lives.

Samson welcomed Delilah, and he died a blind man in the camp of his enemies.

"And the lords of the Philistines came to her and said to her, entice him and see in what his great strength lies, and by what means we may overpower him that we may bind him to subdue him. And we will each give you 1,100 pieces of silver." (Judges 16:5 Amplified Version)

She was on a mission to destroy Samson. There will always be someone close to you on a mission to destroy your dream.

"...but the philistines laid hold of him, bored out his eyes and brought him down to Gaza and bound him with (two) Bronze fetters; and he ground at the mill in prison." (Judges 16:21 Amplified Version)

With the help of the Holy Spirit, there is a need to discern the motives of those who join you as you pursue your God-given dream. The leading cause of failing dreams is wrong associations.

The other category of people will be those God will bring into your life as mentors, amour bearers, and partners. No dream can flourish in isolation. Potiphar welcomed Joseph into his house and all that he had grown.

"...but the lord was with Joseph, and he (Though a slave) was

a successful and prosperous man; and he was in the house of his master the Egyptian. And his master saw that the Lord was with him and made all that he did to flourish and succeed in his hand." (Genesis 39:2-3 Amplified Version)

Laban welcomed Jacob and he prospered:

"And Laban said to him, if I have found favor in your sight, I pray you (do not go); for l have learned by experience and from the omens in divination that the Lord has favored me with blessings on your account." (Genesis 30: 27 Amplified Version)

God intends that when you enter a relationship with someone, they will help you achieve your dreams as you help them achieve theirs.

Pharaoh welcomed Joseph, and his kingdom became the wealthiest:

"And Pharaoh said to him, can we find this man's equal, a man in whom is the Spirit of God?" (Genesis 41:38 Amplified Version)

Some of these relationships are for life, and others are for a season only. As people leave your life, please do not get so stuck with them that you forget the source of the dream. Many have been wounded and fallen by the wayside because somebody walked out of their lives. If that's you, get up, that is not your destination! It's time to rise and move.

"Call to me, and I will answer you and show you great and mighty things, fenced in and hidden, which you do not know (do not distinguish and recognize, have knowledge of and understand)." (Jeremiah 33:3 Amplified Version)

Pray to God whenever men forsake you. He will never walk out of your life. If you walk blameless before him, open doors and more glorious relationships await. You must constantly remember that those who fight or reject you cannot destroy God's dream for you if you fellowship with God through the Holy Spirit.

Constantly cover your dream in prayer and recruit prayer partners; avoid hanging around the wrong people too much. Those you relate with have the potential of breaking or building your plan. Remember that you will always share the rewards and suffer the consequences of those around you. Do not give up on fighting those battles that draw you closer to accomplishing your dream.

Your dream is a magnet that will attract financial resources.

Once people's hearts capture your dream, your dream will have captured their pockets. Few people will have a passion to support you as a person. Many will want to keep or support your vision even long after you have ceased to live. Your dream is not yet successful until you have a successor for it. There must be a Joshua for every Moses.

"AFTER THE death of Moses, the servant of the Lord, the Lord said to Joshua son of Nun, Moses' minister . . ." (Joshua 1:1 Amplified Version)

"And Joshua, son of Nun, was full of the Spirit of wisdom, for Moses had laid his hands upon him; so the Israelites listened to him and did as the Lord commanded Moses." (Deuteronomy 34:9 Amplified Version)

Moses had mentored Joshua.

An Elisha for every Elijah.

"Then Elisha arose and followed and served Elijah..." (1 Kings 19:21b)

What do you think will happen to the dream you are building now when you cease to live? Will your business, ministry, or whatever you are doing now last another generation? Jesus chose his 12 disciples and empowered them to continue with His mission.

"Jesus approached and, breaking the silence, said to them, all authority (all power of rule) in heaven and on earth has been given to Me. Go then and make disciples of all the nations, baptizing them into the name of the Father and of the Son and of the Holy Spirit, teaching them to observe everything that I have commanded you, and behold, I am with you all the days (perpetually, uniformly, and on every occasion), to the [very] close and consummation of the age. Amen (so let it be)." (Matthew 28:18-20 Amplified Version)

- The mission continues through those who are obedient to His command.

Chapter 12

Dreams and Their Cost!

Dreams which do not require faith in God are for ordinary people. Faith is not trying to believe something regardless of the evidence but also daring to do something regardless of the consequences.

"Shadrach, Meshach, and Abednego answered the king: Our God will save us; but if He does not, we will not worship your image." (Daniel 3:16-18 Amplified Version)

The three Hebrew men believed that God was able to save them.

This was the only way they could see the fourth man. When God puts something in your heart, He will not allow you to suffer shame forever if you persevere in faith. If the source of your dream is God, He will give you the grace to accomplish it. It is impossible to tap into the resources of God unless you attempt impossible things for Him. Your confidence should be in the source of the dream.

It Is Impossible to Tap into the Resources of God Unless You Attempt Impossible Things for Him.

"I have strength for all things in Christ who empowers me (am ready for anything and equal to anything through him)" Who infuses inner strength in me; am self-sufficient in Christ sufficiency." (Philippians 14:13 Amplified Version)

Dreams, faith, and risk are triplets. Moses risked the comfort of the palace.

"(Aroused) by faith, Moses when he had grown to maturity and become great, refused to be called the son of pharaoh's daughter because he preferred to share the oppression (suffer the hardships) and bare the shame of the people of God rather than to have the fleeting enjoyment of a sinful life. He considered the contempt and abuse and shame (borne for) the Christ (the messiah who was to come) to be greater wealth than all the treasures of Egypt, for he looked forward and away to the reward (recompense). (motivated) by faith he left Egypt behind him, being unawed and undismayed by the wrath of the king; for he never flinched but he held staunchly to his purpose and endured steadfastly as one who gazed on him who is invisible." (Hebrews 11:24-27 Amplified Version)

The proof of your faith is obedience. Moses sacrificed the comfort of the palace and lived in a desert for 40 years. What a price! Most people will choose comfort over commitment to the dream giver. What is your choice?

Moses Sacrificed the Comfort of the Palace and Lived in a Desert for 40 Years. What a Price!

We are all creatures of comfort and more comfortable with what appeals to our five senses. Successful dreams are built in two dimensions; spiritual and physical.

"Since we consider and look not to the things that are seen

but to the things that are unseen; for the things that are visible are temporal (brief and fleeting, but the things that are invisible are deathless and everlasting)." (2 Corinthians 4:18)

The source of Joseph's dream was a spiritual one, but the physical work for its fulfillment cost him thirteen years of slavery, false accusations, and total isolation from his family.

"He sent a man before them, even Joseph, who was sold as a servant, his feet they hurt with fetters; he was laid in chains of iron and his soul entered in iron until his word, (to his cruel brothers) came true, until the word of the Lord tried and tested him." (Psalm 105:17-19 Amplified Version)

I am glad that when God gives you a dream, He doesn't show you every detail. Otherwise, we would be scared and would not attempt to start on the journey.

FEAR!

Fear is one of the greatest enemies of every dream. Fear of failure is one primary reason why many do not risk obeying God. Fear stifles creativity and reduces productivity. Someone once said that fear is False Evidence Appearing Real. This is true most of the time.

"So, I was afraid, and I went and hid your talent in the ground." Here you have what is your own." (Matthew 25:25 Amplified Version)

Fear made him unproductive. We must learn to turn our failures into positive learning experiences. The greatest mistake many people make is the fear of making mistakes. Fear of failure reduces the willingness to risk. Risk is exposing oneself to the possibility of loss or harm. This fear presents a constant temptation to settle for what has been tried and proven in the past.

The Greatest Mistake Many People Make is the Fear of Making Mistakes.

Jesus' disciples failed repeatedly, yet He continued to give them the task of ministering to people.

"And I brought him to your disciples, and they were not able to cure him." (Matthew 17:16 Amplified Version)

This was a failure on their part. They must have prayed and screamed to the devil, but nothing happened. Have you ever experienced failure in any area of your life? God is not yet through with you and has not given up on you.

"And they went out and preached everywhere while the Lord kept working with them and confirming the message by the attesting signs and miracles that closely accompanied (it). Amen. (So be it)" (Mark 16:20 Amplified Version)

God empowered them, and they changed their world. He is willing to empower you to change your world.

"So now proclaim in the ears of the men, whoever is fearing

and trembling let him turn back and depart from Mount Gilead." (Judges 7:3-8 Amplified Version)

Instead, God would remain with 300 unfearful soldiers rather than with 31,700 who are afraid in their hearts. Fear defeats you before you reach the battlefield.

Whatever Sacrifice God Will Ask You, He Will Provide.

"WHEN YOU go forth to battle against your enemies and see horses and chariots and an army greater than your own, do not be afraid of them for the Lord your God, who brought you out of the land of Egypt, is with you. And when you come near to the battle, the priest shall approach and speak to the men. And shall say to them, hear, O Israel, YOU draw near this day to battle against your enemies. Let not your (minds and) hearts faint; fear not, and do not tremble or be" terrified (and in dread) because of them. For the Lord, your God is He who goes with you to fight for you against your enemies to save you." (Deuteronomy 20:1-4 Amplified Version)

In most cases, your dream will take longer than you expected, may even be more complicated than you anticipated, and more expensive than your thought. That's why many people choose to give up too soon.

Some of the costs are financial (putting in more than you thought), social, emotional, and spiritual, and rejection by those who do not want to associate with you because they do not believe you will succeed or by those who envy your success.

Whatever you will face as you pursue your God-given dream is nothing compared to the anointing you already have. Whatever sacrifice God will ask of you, He will provide. Your only part is to obey.

Chapter 13

Dreams and Giants!

Every dream will have giants or dream killers. This is why you need God on your side since He is bigger than any giant you will ever face. One of the great giants is the tongue, be it your own or others' tongues. Whoever said that insults could not break a bone was wrong.

Words are such a powerful weapon in the hands of the enemy that they can kill our dreams.

Unfortunately, much of this is done by us.

"A man a (moral) self shall be filled with the fruit of his mouth, and with the consequences of his words he must be satisfied (whether good or evil)." Death and life are in the power of the tongue, and they who indulge in it shall eat the fruit of it (for death or life)." (Proverbs 18:20-21 Amplified Version)

"For by your words, you will be justified and acquitted, and by your words, you will be condemned and sentenced." (Matthew 12:37 Amplified Version)

Four examples of destruction by the tongue in the Bible include:
- The negative report by eight spies (Numbers 14:36-37)
- The report of Doeg to King Saul (1 Samuel 22:10-16)
- God's work ceased because of the word of the Samaritans (Ezra 4:4-5)

- Sennacherib's intimidation of God's people. (2 Kings 18:26-27)

Think about the damage words did in these people's lives.

Becoming a believer.

"Because if you acknowledge and confess with your lips that Jesus is Lord and, in your heart, believe (adhere to, trust in, and reply on the truth) that God raised Him from the dead, you will be saved. For with the heart a person believes (adhere to, trust in, and relies on Christ), and so is justified (declared righteous, acceptable to God) and with the mouth he confesses (he declares openly and speaks out freely his faith) and confirms (his) salvation." (Romans 10:9-10 Amplified Version)

"For let him who wants to enjoy life and see good days (good-whether apparent or not) keep his tongue free from evil and his lips from guile (treachery, deceit)." (1 Peter 3:10 Amplified Version)

This shows two kinds of tongues and destinies.

"Truthful lips shall be established forever, but a lying tongue is (credited), but for a moment." (Proverbs12:19 Amplified Version)

Have you noticed that you have two eyes to see with, two ears to hear with, and only a tongue covered with two lips and fenced with 32 teeth? Assuming you still have a complete set!

Your conversation reveals whether you are a winner or a loser. Losers major in problems and obstacles, while winners discuss possibilities and opportunities.

"Caleb quieted the people before Moses, and said, let us go up at once and possess it; we are well able to conquer it." (Numbers 13:30 Amplified Version)

Have you ever noticed that when you greet some people, they begin with "Oh I had a sleepless night", I had a bad dream, etc." Few will tell you how thankful they are that they are alive and have shelter over their head. They always emphasize what is wrong. You must start praising God for what you already have. Concentrate on your victories and worship God regardless of your current circumstances.

Your Conversation Reveals Whether You Are a Winner or a Loser.

"Though the fig tree does not blossom and there is no fruit on the vines, though the product of the olive fails, and the fields yield no food, though the flock is cut off from the fold and there are no cattle in the stalls. Yet I will rejoice in the Lord; I will exult in (the victorious) God of my salvation! The Lord God is my strength, my personal bravery, and my invincible army; He makes my feet like hinds' feet and will make me to walk (not to stand still in terror, but to walk) and make (spiritual) progress upon my high places (of trouble, suffer in ore responsibility)." (Habakkuk 3:17-19 Amplified Version)

Ezekiel 37 tells a story of dry bones. Read the story and you will notice the prophet's part in this miracle. He spoke what God told him to speak.

Practice speaking God's word over every area of your life regularly, and you will be amazed at the power of words.

Close to our headquarters was a piece of land we desired to add to our ministry land. However, we needed the funds to purchase it. A Muslim man bought it and began building a big house. It was a two- in one bungalow. As he was building, we began to pray, telling God we were not ready to fight battles with the Muslim since his home would be less than five meters from the church. The prayer was, "Lord, give us this property." The man steadily built this house up to the ring beam. We did not waver but continued to pray, walk around the place, and claim it.

"Ask of me, and I will give you the nation as your inheritance, and the uttermost parts of the earth as your possession." (Psalm 2:8 Amplified Version)

We were reminding God of His willingness to give us the nations of the world, but now we are praying for a tiny piece of land. After some time, the man stopped building and disappeared. Later we saw people coming in big cars to look at his property. The owner had decided to sell it, but we did not know. But even after knowing this, we had no money to buy. We prayed against any plan by anybody to buy it. One day God gave us the money, and I looked for the property owner. He said, "Now I know your God answers prayers; because I lost all interest in that property." I have built and finished two other houses, but I do not know what happened with that property. I think your God preserved it for you." In my heart, I was shouting halleluiah!

We kept the dream in our hearts and never gave up on praying. We named the building The Dream House.

Enemies.

Every dream has a supernatural ability to attract opposition right from the beginning. I am convinced that your enemies are as necessary as your friends. Friends provide comfort; enemies offer promotion. They turn nobodies into somebodies. The secret here is fighting the enemy God's way. When facing an enemy against your dream, know the battle is not yours but God's.

"The Lord says this to you: be not afraid or dismayed at this great multitude; for the battle is not yours, but God's." (2 Chronicles 20:15b)

Never allow your enemy to dictate over God's word or promise to you.

"And they rose early in the morning and went out into the Wilderness of Tekoa; and as they went out, Jehoshaphat stood and said, hear me, O Judah, and you inhabitants of Jerusalem believe in the lord your God and you shall be established; believe and remain steadfast to His prophets and you shall prosper." (2 Chronicles 20:20 Amplified Version)

The enemy's strategy is to intimidate you, but never let fear or past pain stop you from setting new goals. Your dream's destiny will require you to overcome fear even when outnumbered.

You must make up your mind not to dwell on the negative: you must renew your mind and be a good prophet to your dream: stop beating yourself; you can be your biggest enemy.

Stop Beating Yourself; You Can Be Your Biggest Enemy.

Common enemies to every dream include:

Ego, fear of failure/success, lack of self–esteem, procrastination, giving up your dream for the promise of money, lack of training, persistence, lack of priorities, lack of focus, lack of planning...the list is endless.

Remember: He has made us more than conquerors in Christ.

Chapter 14

Relationships!

Without dreams, people perish, and without people, dreams perish!

Apart from God, the Source of your dream, people are a priority; they are the greatest resource for every dream. Natural talent, charisma, and excellent education, none guarantee a successful dream.

Other peoples' skills and talents are essential for every dream. The people that you relate with have the potential of helping to build or to break your dream. Satan is in constant negotiation for your destiny-and he will bring anybody into your life to sabotage you. He will bring somebody into your life whenever God wants to bless your dream. Your success involves other people.

I rarely go fishing, but l have never caught a fish without dropping a hook and bait. The bait attracts the attention of the fish. It is something they love. Satan constantly falls bait in your pond of life.

Without Dreams, People Perish, and Without People, Dreams Perish.

Nobody will wake up with a successful dream in isolation. It is essential that you choose who speaks into your life.

First of all, allow God's word to speak to you daily.

Goliath never killed a single Israelite. He used words to intimidate Israel for forty days.

"When Saul and all Israel heard those words of the Philistines, they were dismayed and greatly afraid." (1 Samuel 17:11 Amplified Version)

Samson heeded Delilah daily; he died a blind man after revealing the secret of his power to her.

"...when she pestered him daily with her words and pressed him...he told her all his heart." (Judges 16:16)

Joseph in Genesis behaved differently when confronted with Potiphar's wife.

"She spoke to Joseph day after day, but he didn't listen to her, to lie with her or to be with her." (Genesis 39:10 Amplified Version)

Potiphar's wife begged him daily for sex. He chose to run away. What would have happened if Joseph had yielded? I am not sure he would not have gone to prison where he met a prisoner who linked him to the king.

His wife advised Job to curse God and die. He chose not to, and God rewarded him for that.

"Then his wife said to him, do you still hold fast your blame-

less uprightness? Renounce God and die." (Job 2:9: Amplified Version)

Whenever you associate with the wrong people, their words will play a vital part in destroying your dream. All great dreams have been built by teams of people. Think about your most significant achievements in life so far and about your greatest downfall. How many things happened to you when you were alone? To build a great dream, you must learn the art of initiating and investing in solid relationships. There are many suitable initiators of relationships but who need to improve at maintaining them.

If you want to befriend people, the starting point is being friendly yourself. Do you have any people you want to have a chance to meet? Why would you like to meet them? Can they open some doors for you if you meet them? How would you like them to treat you when and after you meet them? If you are going to build relationships, treat others the way you would want the people you admire to treat you.

If You Want to Befriend People, the Starting Point is Being Friendly Yourself.

When we respect people regardless of their status, they will want to return to us.

We must learn to respect people not because they deserve it but because we want to be treated the same way someday.

When you learn to respect and befriend people, you will meet and make friends wherever you go. The saying is true: the likable person still wins all things being or not being equal.

John Maxwell says:
- People are insecure-give them confidence.
- People want to feel special; Sincerely complement them.
- People desire a better tomorrow - show them hope.
- People get emotionally low - encourage them.
- People are selfish - speak to their needs first.
- People want to be associated with success - help them win.

When you help others achieve their dreams, your dream is guaranteed success.

Charles Spurgeon says, *curve your name on hearts, not on marble.*

What can you do to improve your relationships? Put others first, be patient with them, see the best in them, serve them, and be generous to them. That is what Jesus did.

"For even the Son of Man came not to have service rendered to him, but to serve, and to give his life as a ransom for (instead of) many." (Mark 10:45: Amplified Version)

God did not create you with friends but gave you time, talent, and treasure, which you can invest in people to make friends. Your dreams will never be nurtured by someone whose dreams are smaller than yours. Hence the importance of having a mentor in your life. This should be someone who has been where you want to go. People who have been where you want to go will only have opinions about how you should get there.

"BLESSED (Happy, fortunate, prosperous, and enviable) is the man who waits and lives not in the counsel of the ungodly (following their advice, their plans and purpose), nor stands (submissive and inactive) in the path where sinners walk, nor sits down (to relax and rest) where the scornful (and the mockers) gather." (Psalm 1:1 Amplified Version)

According to the above scriptures, your dream will require you to work with others, but not all people. Your dream will be advanced through temporary as much as permanent relationships. It would be best to guard your temporary and permanent relationships because your enemy cannot defeat your dream unless he sabotages the relationships that sustain your dreams.

However, none of those you relate with should be permitted to control or own you. Those that want to grow with you will never want to isolate you by owning you. You must learn to treasure every relationship as if the destiny of your dream depended on them but never replace those relationships with the dream Giver.

We must have the right attitude about the people who relate to us, whether we are under their authority or vice versa. Always ask yourself: "Am I building people, or am I building my dream using people to do it?"

To be a good steward of a God–given dream, do not move together with others for your advantage. This is equally true in Christian ministries, businesses, homes, and politics. People's greatest fear is being manipulated, which is a form of witchcraft. No one wants to feel used!

People's Greatest Fear is Being Manipulated, Which is a Form of Witchcraft.

Nothing can be compared with teamwork.

"And the Lord said, behold, they are ONE PEOPLE, and they have all ONE LANGUAGE; this is only the beginning of what they will do, and now nothing they have imagined they can do will be impossible for them." (Genesis 11:6 Amplified Version)

The team spirit of these people gets God's attention. Had it not been for the wrong motive behind their dream, I am sure they would succeed. Think about where you have come from and where you are now. Whether positively or negatively, your achievements or losses have involved other people. Every dreamer must choose people to counsel with.

"Where no wise guidance is, the people fall, but in the multitude of counselors there is safety." (Proverbs 11:14 Amplified Version)

Our dreams will move further when we propose to build solid relationships. As I have mentioned earlier, you must be a person of good character. No one wants to relate with people who will embarrass them. You must know that your character is the oil that allows you to connect well with other people without friction.

If you want to relate well with other people, get to know their dreams, do your best to help them achieve them, and they will automatically want to connect with you. We must relate with all people but must choose our friends carefully.

Some people think the best way to help others is by criticizing them. Purpose to be different by encouraging others. Build your reputation as an encourager.

Moses had Joshua, Aaron, and Hur.

"But Moses' hands were heavy and grew weary. So (the other men) took a stone and put it under him, and he sat on it. Then Aaron and Hur held up his hands, one on one side and one on the other side; so his hands were steady until the going down of the sun." (Exodus 17:12 Amplified Version)

You must read from verse eight to get the whole story. Although Moses was God's anointed and displayed tremendous power through him in Egypt, he still needed Aaron and Hur as partners. That is how they defeated the Amalekites. Do you have any "ites" in your life? I am talking about poverty-ites, barren-ites, you need partners to hold you in prayer.

Daniel had shadrach, Meshach and Abednego.

"Then Daniel went to his house and made the thing known

to Hananiah, Mishael, and Azariah, his companions, that they might seek mercies from God of heaven concerning the secret so that Daniel and his companions should not perish with the rest of the wise men of Babylon." (Daniel 2:17-18)

Jesus had the 12, then the three, Peter, James, and John.

"AND SIX days after this, Jesus took with him Peter and James and John his brother and led them up on a high mountain by themselves." (Matthew 17:1 Amplified Version)

Who are the people in the inner circle of your dream?

Chapter 15

Pillars of Strength Against Giants!

1. Character

This is what you are when no one is looking. These are the moral qualities that make you. We must choose to be the best we can be for God, pursue the highest values, and live according to those values. The enemy will always seek to assassinate your character to destroy your dream. Unfortunately, many people only care about their public image or what they want people to think of them. Character is like a tree, and reputation is like a shadow. I would rather be a tree.

"BLESSED (HAPPY, fortunate, prosperous, and enviable) is the man who walks and lives not in the counsel of the ungodly (following their advice, their plans where sinners walk, nor sits down (to relax and rest) where the scornful (and the mockers) gather. But his delight and desire are in the law of the Lord, and on his law (the precepts, the instructions, the teachings of God), he habitually meditates (ponders and studies) by day and by night. And he shall be like a tree firmly planted (and tended) by the streams of water, ready to bring forth its fruit in its season; its leaf also shall not fade or wither; and everything he does shall prosper (and come to maturity)." (Psalm 1:1-3 Amplified Version)

Character is like steel in a concrete pillar. It is invisible from the outside, but the building cannot stand the storms without that steel. It is said that character at home is kindness; in business, it is honesty and helps the weak. It is resistance to the wicked. It is forgiveness towards the penitent, reverence, and love towards God. The character has to shine through everything we do and speak. It is better to be short of money than to be short of character.

"A good name is rather to be chosen than great riches and loving rather than silver and gold." (Proverbs 22:1)

Talent and skill may take you to a palace, but your character will determine how long you stay there. Everybody can be praised for their gift, talents, and skills, but people will only respect you for your character. A young man was about to be promoted at his place of work because everybody thought highly of him. One day while in a restaurant, his supervisor, who had recommended the promotion, saw this young man stealing a piece of butter. The supervisor later withdrew his recommendation. The young man lost the promotion, although he was not told why! Some people will not confront you but will only withdraw or withhold opportunities from you.

2. Courage

This quality lets people control the fear of danger, pain, and misfortune. Being loud and aggressive does not mean that one is courageous. True courage is when we have faith in God. Hebrews chapter 11 is a beautiful chapter that will show how faith in God brought victory after victory to those who believed in God; think about Daniel.

"Now when Daniel knew that the writing was signed, he went into his house, and his windows being open in his chamber towards Jerusalem, he got down his knees three times a day and prayed and gave thanks before his God, as he had done previously." (Daniel 6:10 Amplified Version)

Daniel was thrown into the lion's den. The following day he walked out and was thrown into the same den and their families. None of them survived.

"Then these (three) men were bound in their cloaks., their tunics or undergarments, their turbans, and their other clothing, and they were cast into the midst of the burning fiery furnace. Therefore, because the king's commandment was urgent and the furnace exceeding hot, the flame and sparks from the fire killed those men who handled Shadrach, Meshach, and Abednego, the three fell down bound into the burning fiery furnace." (Daniel 3:21-22 Amplified Version)

The fourth man was already waiting for them in the fire. They walked out of the fire alive: I know the fourth man is still in life's fires waiting for a courageous human being who completely trusts him. No lion, no fire can consume your dream if the source of your courage is God's word. Most of the early Christians in the New Testament, who turned their world upside down, did not die a normal death. Most had a chance of denying their faith amid severe persecution but chose to die physically because of their faith.

"Others had to suffer the trial of the mocking and scourging and even chains and imprisonment. They were stoned to death; they were lured with tempting offers (to renounce their faith): they were sawn asunder; they were slaughtered by the sword; (while they were alive) they had to go about wrapped in the skins of sheep and goats, utterly destitute, oppressed, cruelly treated. (Men) of whom the world was not worthy roaming over the desolate places and the mountains and (living in caves and caverns and holes of the earth)." (Hebrews 11:35b-38 Amplified Version)

3. Commitment

This is a pledge binding oneself. Our commitment must first be to God and our life's authorities and responsibilities. The mistake many make is thinking of God last and only concentrating on daily activities. If you are too busy to show your commitment to God as a priority through praise, worship, prayer, and reading his word, then you are too busy to have a successful dream. Many find it easier to show their commitment to God only when they are in trouble. Imagine you have a child or relative; how many of you will be so caring when you get a call or visit from them when they have problems? Imagine never hearing from them about their new jobs, new house, new car, wedding ceremonies, or graduation party, and the only time you hear from them is when they are thinking of divorce, suicide, or anything along those lines!

"However, after a long time (nearly forty years) the king of Egypt died; and the Israelites were sighing and groaning because of the bondage. They kept crying, and their cry because of slavery ascended to God." (Exodus 2:23 Amplified Version)

They had been in peaceful slavery for 400 years and never called upon God. The good news is that whenever you call upon him, he hears and sets in motion your deliverance. Maybe you are reading this book, and you need help. Perhaps you have been like the prodigal son in Luke 15. God is right there with you. Repentance brings Him closer to your heart, and you can renew your relationship.

"Behold, I stand at the door and knock if anyone hears and listens to and heeds my voice and opens the door, I will come into him and will eat with him, and he (will eat) with me." (Revelation 3:20 Amplified Version)

The above scripture shows how close you are to having Christ. If He is not at the center of your life and you have welcomed other things that you know are sins before God, why do not you ask him to come into your life right now?

4. Conviction

It is a firm assured belief. If you cannot stand for anything, you can fall for anything. For your dream to come to pass, you must have boundaries over your life.

"But Daniel determined in his heart that he would not defile himself by (eating his portion of) the king's rich and dainty food or by (drinking) the wine which he drank; therefore, he requested of the chief of the eunuchs that he might (be allowed) not to defile himself." (Daniel 1:8 Amplified Version)

Daniel set his values at the beginning. No wonder he succeeded in all things. If you want to succeed in God's way, God's word must set the boundaries for you. Obedience to God's wants equals life, blessing, health, and prosperity.

"You cannot drink the Lord's cup and the demon's cup. You cannot partake of the Lord's table and the demon's table." (1 Corinthians 10:21: Amplified Version)

"If you are willing and obedient, you shall eat the good of the land; but if you refuse and rebel, you will be devoured by the sword. For the mouth of the Lord has spoken it." (Isaiah 1:19-20 Amplified Version)

"If you will listen diligently to the voice of the Lord your God, being watchful to do all His commandments which I command you this day, the Lord your God will set you high above all the nations of the earth. And all these blessings shall come upon you and overtake you if you heed the voice of the Lord your God." (Deuteronomy 28:15 Amplified Version)

Disobedience to God is equated to poverty, curses, disease, and death.

Our love and devotion to God must be the foundation for successful dreams. The destiny of your dream depends on who sets your boundaries, God, Satan, yourself, or others. You cannot be blessed beyond your last act of obedience. However, you must obey instructions. The word instruction means correction, discipline, and warning. It includes all forms of discipline intended to lead to a transformed life. God cannot be the source of your success if He is not the source of your standard.

This calls for spending time with God in prayer and the Word and fellowship with God's people. You lose credibility the moment you change sides from purity to popularity—people who spend as much time accommodating your enemy as they do, you have no conviction. Having conviction means you are not ashamed of where you stand. People without conviction for your dream want the benefit of knowing you without the commitment of guarding you and your dream.

"And this is why am suffering as I do. Still am not ashamed, for I know (perceive, have knowledge of, and am acquainted with) Him Whom I have believed (adhered to and trusted in and relied on), and I am (positively) persuaded that He is able to guard and keep that which has been entrusted to me and which I have committed (to Him) until that day." (2 Timothy 1:12)

"For I'm not ashamed of the gospel (good news) of Christ, for it is God's power working unto salvation (for deliverance from eternal death) to everyone who believes with a personal trust and a confident surrender and firm reliance, to the Jew and also to the Greek." (Romans 1:16 Amplified Version)

Only a few people have suffered like Apostle Paul for their assignments, but Paul never gave up. He finished the race.

"But arise and stand upon your feet; for I have appeared to you for this purpose, that I might appoint you to serve as

(My) Minister and to bear witness both to what you have seen of me and to that in which I will appear to you. Choosing you out (Selecting you for myself) And delivering you from among the (Jewish) people and the Gentiles to whom am sending to you. To open their eyes that they may turn from darkness to light and from the power of Satan to God, so that they may thus receive forgiveness and release from their sins and the place and portion among those- who are consecrated and purified by faith in me. Wherefore, O King Agrippa, I was not disobedient onto the heavenly vision." (Acts 26-16-19 Amplified Version)

5. Courtesy

This is the way you treat other people. It is having and showing good manners, being polite and kind. Whenever you treat people right, even those who think they do not deserve it, you are sowing for being treated right whenever you need it or even for your offspring. Jonathan treated David right, and when Jonathan died, David looked for Mephibosheth, Jonathan's son, and treated him well.

"Then Jonathan made a covenant with David because he loved him as his own life. And Jonathan stripped himself of the robe that was on him and gave it to David, and his armor, even his sword, his bow, and his girdle." (1 Samuel 18:3-4 Amplified Version)

1 Samuel 20 shows Jonathan's loyalty to David.

"AND DAVID, said, is there still anyone left of the house of

Saul to whom I may show kindness for Jonathan's sake?" (2 Samuel 9: 1 Amplified Version)

David repays kindness to Jonathan's offspring.

These are pillars that you cannot build in a day. We must constantly work on these areas.

Persistence in each of these areas will bring success to our dreams. Regardless of how far the destination is, make up your mind and press toward the goal.

It is a waste of time to try to achieve what someone you admire has if you are unwilling to do what they did to achieve it. Successful dreams result from decisions and discipline as much as hard work and handling relationships correctly.

Never defend the blessings your dream yields to a critic who refuses to understand what you endured to reach your level. Someone who doesn't know where you came from will never understand your dream.

Jesus Christ commanded us to treat others the way we want to be treated.

Chapter 16

Dreams and Prayers!

You are here on purpose, designed and equipped for a particular assignment. Talents and gifts are given to us by God but in raw form. The more time you spend in His presence, the more you will be sharpened to realize your dreams.

Jeremiah 33:3 - **"Call on me in prayer, and I will answer you. I will show you great and mighty things which you still do not know about."**

Your dream is as strong or as weak as your prayer life. Life is about becoming. Many people desire to become doctors, lawyers, pastors, police officers, etc., but you can become all that and still be empty and unhappy if you do not have a relationship with God through Christ.

"And Jesus said to them, come after me and be my disciples, and I will make you to become fishers of men." (Mark 1:17 Amplified Version)

The above Scripture talks about having a relationship with Jesus before being empowered to become. Like the missing puzzle piece, life only makes sense once He is included. The God connection is the bridge from failing to succeeding in your dream.

If there is anything I have learned from God is that everything flows out of one's relationship with the Lord. Our private life with God is more important than our public life. Also, whatever is birthed through prayer can only be preserved by worship. Prayer is declared in the Bible to be of overwhelming importance.

The outstanding people of God in both the Old and the New Testament were characterized by much prayer, including Jesus Himself. Anything of value in the kingdom of God is initiated by and is dependent upon prayer.

An invitation to pray:

"Let us then fearlessly and confidently and boldly draw near to the throne of grace (the throne of God's unmerited favor to us sinners) that we may receive mercy (for our failures) and find grace to help in good tie for every need (appropriate help and well – timed help, coming just when we need it.") (Hebrews 4:16 Amplified Version)

"Be unceasing in prayer (praying perseveringly.) (1 Thessalonians 5:17 Amplified Version)

We are living in dangerous times, and if there was ever a time when we needed to pray for our dreams, it is now. Efficient prayer comes from obedience. When we pray about our dreams, God will give us instructions. Obedience to those instructions then yields an increase in our dreams.

Unfortunately, some people are too busy praying to hear God speak to them.

Many praying people complain that God doesn't speak to them; they are like Samuel.

"Now Samuel did not yet know the Lord, and the word of the Lord wasn't revealed to him." (1Samuel 3:7 Amplified Version)

God called him, but he was not mature enough to discern His voice from Eli's.

"So, Samuel grew, and the Lord was with him and let none of his words fall to the ground, then the Lord appeared to him, and revealed Himself to Samuel by the word." (1 Samuel 3:19-21)

He could discern God's word after he had grown in the Lord.

Prayerlessness is telling God you can manage your dream without him. It is pride.

Pride is a giant step away from God and brings you one step closer to your failure. Those below you will always enjoy your failure and only find significance in your loss of position.

To stay on top of your dream, stay on top of the mountain and deny them a chance to rejoice over you.

"And Moses said to Joshua, choose us out men and go out, fight with Amalek. Tomorrow l will stand on top of the hill with the rod of God in my hand. So, Joshua did as Moses said and fought with Amalek and, Moses, Aaron and went

up to the hilltop. When Moses held up his hand, Israel prevailed, and when he lowered his hand, Amalek prevailed."
(Exodus 17:8-11 Amplified Version)

This shows that Israel's victory depended on the prayerful-
ness of Moses on the mountain top. Are you experiencing defeat in some areas of your life? You need to spend more time
with God. Get prayer partners like Moses did when Aron and
Hur held his hands.

Temptations:

Temptation is anything that attracts you away from God's
principles.

The last petition in the Lord's prayer:

"...And bring us not into temptations but rescue as from
evil." (Luke 11:4b Amplified Version)

It is a prayer to God for strength to withstand moral perils so
that we do not fail or be overwhelmed by the evil one.

When our dreams fail, it is always easier to blame other people or circumstances beyond our control. But the temptations
people fall into are the primary cause of why dreams don't
come to pass. As I have mentioned earlier, keeping ourselves
in prayer is the solution.

"All of you must keep awake (give strict attention and be ac-
tive) and watch and pray that you may not come into temp-

tation. The spirit indeed is willing, but the flesh is weak."
(Matthew 26:41 Amplified Version)

"Simon, Simon, (Peter), listen! Satan has asked excessively
that (all of) you be given up to him (out of the power and
keeping of God) that he might sift (all of) you like grains.
"But I have prayed especially for you (Peter) that your own
faith may not fail, and when you yourself have turned again,
strengthen and establish your brethren." (Luke 22:31-32
Amplified Version)

Temptation is not a sin, but yielding to it is. I view temptation
as choosing temporary gain, pleasure, and shortcuts to prosperity, marriage, etc. All dreamers have come to this turning
point in their lives. The choices they made led to tragedy or
triumph in their lives.

Samson was born for an assignment, God's dream for his life.

"For behold, you shall become pregnant and bear a son. No
razor shall come upon his head, for the child shall be a Na-
zirite to God from birth, and he shall begin to deliver Israel
out of the hands of the Philistines." (Judges 13:5 Amplified
Version)

Delilah enticed him daily until he yielded to this temptation.
Samson died a blind man.

David gave occasion to the enemies of the Lord because he
yielded to the temptation of adultery and murder.

"One evening David arose from his couch and was walking on the roof of the king's house when he saw a woman bathing, and she was very lovely behold". 2 Sam 11:2

"Nevertheless, because by his deed you have utterly scorned the Lord and given great occasion to the enemies of the Lord to blaspheme, the child that is born to you shall surely die." (2 Samuel 12:14 Amplified Version)

Observing what happens when someone yields to temptation makes you want to be like Joseph, who refused to sin with Potiphar's wife, or like Daniel and his three friends in captivity, who refused to fall into the temptation of eating food offered to idols. No wonder God promoted them to a foreign land.

"But Daniel determined in his heart that he would not defile himself by eating his portion of the king's rich and dainty food or by (drinking) the wine which he drank; therefore, he requested of the chief of the eunuchs that he might (he allowed) not to defile himself." (Daniel 1:8 Amplified Version)

They refused to obey the king because his decree was against God's word.

Daniel 3:8 and Genesis 39:7-12 tell the rest of the respective stories.

Joseph was tempted daily by Potiphar's wife, but his response was, "1 cannot sin against my God." "He said, "No" and ended up in prison (Genesis 39). But why? You would expect that when you say no to temptation, God will immediately bring a breakthrough.

I would instead go to prison for righteousness than go there because of yielding to temptation.

"So too the (Holy) Spirit comes to our aid and bears us up in our weakness, for we do not know what prayer to offer or how to offer it worthily as we ought, but the Spirit Himself goes to meet our supplication and pleads in our behalf with unspeakable yearnings and groanings too deep for utterance." (Romans 8:26: Amplified Version)

The above Scripture reveals that we can only pray effectively with the help of the Holy Spirit. We must embrace Him as our Teacher and Helper in this great prayer principle if we are to realize our dreams.

I think Joseph had to go to prison. Otherwise, he would not have met the prisoner who linked him to Pharaoh.

So, if you are suffering today because of your godly values and principles, God is about to surprise you with a promotion. I'm sure that Potiphar's wife was laughing because it looked like she had won in her scheme but not for long. It must have been a great surprise to her when she heard that Joseph was now the prime minister of her country.

I Would Rather Go to Prison for Righteousness Than to Go Because of Yielding to Temptation.

Whenever you are tempted to yield to the lust of the flesh,

eyes, and pride of life, think about the consequences before you yield. If you make this a principle, you will save yourself much trouble and enjoy many triumphs.

What happens if you have already yielded to temptation? Remember Samson. Although he was already blind and in the hands of his enemies, God gave him another chance. He made a memorable prayer which God honored.

"Then Samson called to the Lord and said, O Lord God, (earnestly) remember me, I pray you and strengthen me, I pray you, only this once, O God, and let me have one vengeance upon the Philistines for both my eyes." (Judges 16:28 Amplified Version)

Also, remember Prophet Jonah, whom a whale swallowed. Even in the belly of a fish, when he cried to God, He honored his prayer. Even while attending Whale University, Jonah 2 shows one of the most wonderful prayers.

You are not so much of a sinner that God cannot hear you. He can restore what you lost. Take some time and read the story of the prodigal son in Luke 15. Also, read Psalm 51. If you are currently in the middle of many temptations, look to God; there is always a way of escape.

"For no temptation (no trial regarded as enticing to sin) (no matter how it comes or where it leads) has overtaken you and laid hold on you that is not common to man (that is, no temptation or trial has come to you that is beyond human resistance and that is not adjusted and adapted and

belonging to human experience and such as man can bear). But God is faithful (to His Word and to His compassionate nature), and He (can be trusted) not to let you be tempted and tried and assayed beyond your ability and strength of resistance and power to endure, but with the temptation He will (always) also provide the way out (the means of escape to a landing place), that you may be capable and strong and powerful to bear up under it patiently." (1Corinthians 10:13 Amplified Version)

As a compass needle is affected by magnetic attraction, so every Christian feels the pull of sin daily. Consider the Israelites' desire to return to the leeks and garlic of Egypt after seeing God's miracles in Exodus 16. Think of Paul's fellow minister:

"For Demas has deserted me for love of this present world and has gone to Thessalonica; Crescens (has gone) to Galatia, Titus to Dalmatia." (2 Timothy 4:10 Amplified Version)

I wonder how it must have felt to have Paul as a leader, watching the exploits that God did through him. For these people to desert him for the world, that must have been a strong pull of the world. If Satan could do this to Paul's close friends, he would want to do the same in our lives.

A sense of achievement and assurance always results from victory over temptation.

Dreamers are not exempted from the temptation of giving in to discouragement, despair, and resentment toward those who have caused them problems in the past. Let Joseph be your example whenever you are tempted to be discouraged and resentful.

"Then, after a time his master's wife cast her eyes upon Joseph, and she said, Lie with me. But he refused and said to his master's wife, see here, with me in the house my master has concern about nothing. He has put all that he has in my care." (Genesis 39:7-8 Amplified Version)

Satan uses the same tricks, enticing us with the lust of the flesh, the lust of the eyes, and the pride of life.

"For all that is in the world-the lust of the flesh (craving for sensual gratification) and the lust of the eyes (greedy longings of the mind) and the pride of Life (assurance in one's own resources or in the stability of earthly things) – these do not come from the Father but are from the world (itself). And the world passes away and disappears, and with it the forbidden cravings (the passionate desires, the lust) of it; but he who does the will of God and carries out His purposes in his life abides (remains) forever." (1 John 2:16-17 Amplified Version)

I see temptation as poison coated with sugar that the devil gives you to eat. He will always time you when you are hungry.

Temptation is a choice between an immediate temporary pleasure and an eternal gain - if you wait a little longer. The two greatest pains people will always live with are regret and discipline. I would rather live with the pain of discipline; what about you? Ask Samson, and he will testify that a moment of pleasure with Delilah was not worth dying a blind man.

Let us look at a moment in David's life.

"One evening David arose from his couch and was walking on the roof of the king's house when from there he saw a woman bathing, and she was very lovely to behold." (2Samuel 11:2 Amplified Version)

Consequences:

"Now therefore, the sword shall never depart from your house because by this deed you have utterly scorned the Lord and given great occasion to the enemies of the Lord to blaspheme." (v.14 Amplified Version)

Dreams crash daily on the rocks of temptations. Prisons are full of people with extraordinary dreams but who never said "No" to temptation. Many dreams have hit because of the search for fame and glamour. Others yield to illicit sex, searching for favor, money, and success, only to suffer an untimely death.

Our decisions create and control most of our circumstances. The good news is that Jesus came to unhook us from the baits and sins of Satan. Maybe you have made many mistakes, and your dream of a happy family, a thriving business, and an effective ministry has been crushed! Jesus is still in the restoration business; call upon Him now!

"And I will restore or replace for you the years that the locust has eaten-the hopping locust, the stripping locust, and the crawling locust, My great army which I sent among you." (Joel 2:25 Amplified Version)

After repenting, learn to get over the past. God has already taken care of that. Concentrate on rebuilding the dream. Turn your past mistake into positive learning experiences.

Chapter 17

Suffering and Adversity!

Why me? Why my family? Why my business? Why my ministry?"

I am sure you have ever asked yourself a question along those lines! None of us is immune to suffering and adversity. Every dreamer's life has pressures of want, need, sorrow, persecution, unpopularity, and loneliness. Some suffer for what they have done; others suffer because of what people have done to them. Many suffer because they are victims of circumstances beyond their control. What category do you fall under? There will be nights of agony when God seems so unfair, and there is no possible help or answer.

In times of adversity, the solution is not to quit on the dream for your life but to stay in fellowship with God. More people are destroyed by prosperity rather than adversity. What will you do in the face of suffering to learn from it and use it to your advantage as far as God's dream for you is concerned?

If you suffer because of your God-given dream, you will get more blessings if you look to your heavenly Father during agony and despair. Adversity and persecutions are always the last stage before promotion.

"So come on now, let us kill him and throw his body into some pit; then we will say (to our father), some wild and ferocious animal has devoured him, and we shall see what

will become of his dream!" (Genesis 37:20 Amplified Version)

If your adversity or crisis were meant to kill you, God would never leave you in it longer than you can bear. That is why you have survived many plots intended to destroy you. Or maybe your education, ministry, marriage, and business dream were destroyed!

Whatever you have left in your hand is not the matter's conclusion if you are still breathing. The challenge is how you can use what you have to move on. Take some time to read and study 1 Kings 17:8-17.

This portion discusses a widow and her son who were a meal away from death. The little left became the capital or source of sustenance through the famine period. She and her son never lacked food throughout the famine because she obeyed God's instructions.

Read and study 2 Kings 4:1-6.

This portion talks about a widow who was in severe debt. Her sons were about to be taken as slaves. She had only a small jar of oil. She obeyed Elisha's instructions, and she was saved. You might be thinking, "Those at least had something to be able to exercise their faith."

The Biblical truth is that our deliverance will always be within reach in times of desperation. God will not fail us as we pray and consult with people of faith.

"However, in order not to give offense and cause them to stumble (that is to cause them to judge unfavorably and unjustly), go down to the sea and throw in a hook. Take the first fish that comes up, and when you open its mouth, you will find there a shekel. Take it and give it to them to pay the temple tax for me and for yourself." (Matthew 17:27 Amplified Version)

Peter had nothing when the tax collectors came. He obeyed Jesus' word. Whether you have little or nothing, if you have some faith as little as a mustard seed, that is all you need to overcome in your time of desperation.

When Pressure and Tension are Removed from Your Dream, Death Will Follow.

When I was young, my chicken stayed with me in my bedroom. A time came for it to hatch her eggs. I looked at the cracks on the eggs that had not hatched yet and heard the little chicks making noise. I took pity on them and decided to help them out of their shells so they would no longer have to struggle. Shortly afterward, they died.

It is the law of nature that the struggle to come out of the shell helps to develop and strengthen their lungs and wings. I had deprived the chicks of their battle, and they died. Sometimes what we do to help people cripples them when they refuse to take personal responsibility to pursue the dream God has given them.

People who have overcome obstacles are stronger and more

secure than those who have never faced them. The answer to obstacles in your God-given dream is perseverance. Giving up because of suffering and adversity is a permanent solution to a temporary problem.

Chapter 18

Finishing Strong!

Many people are great starters but poor finishers. The only thing that differentiates you from what others start is what you complete. No one has the right to expect prosperity from something they are unwilling to stretch in. Many dreamers have failed because they are unwilling to invest in their dreams.

Read and study Genesis 41:15b.

Pharaoh dreamed of seven years of plenty and seven years of famine. He invested for seven years to overcome the seven years of famine. How have you prepared for your future?

No Finishing Without Self-Discipline.

The saying is true: "Pay now and play later" or "Play now and pay later!" The latter pay is more expensive, maybe not in terms of money, but in terms of pain and regret. Discipline is achieving what you want by doing things you do not want to do now. After doing this for some time, discipline becomes the choice of achieving what you want by doing something you do not want to do now.

D.L. Moody said *I have had more trouble with D.L. Moody than with any other man.*

Looking back, Jack Paar Live said *that my life seems to be one long obstacle with me as the main obstacle.*

Most dreamers fail due to inner rather than outer issues. This could be a lack of self-discipline in dealing with the opposite sex, handling finances, controlling emotions like anger, or anything that they secretly give their eyes and ears to.

The saying is true: *"When we are foolish, we want to conquer the world." When we are wise, we want to conquer ourselves."*

Maybe you have tried to conquer your lack of discipline in vain. Perhaps externally, people admire you, but inwardly you think, "I hope no one will ever know the real me!" Stop impressing others, allow God to work in your life, whatever your dream is, and build a disciplined life.

Make a habit of doing it NOW! We have all procrastinated at some moment in our lives. A complicated task is fulfilling; an incomplete task drains energy like a leak from a tank.

If you want to build your dream, practice the habit of doing it now! Procrastinators always hide behind words like; I am still analyzing it or praying about it!

Remember that we have only one life to live on earth, and you are not getting any younger.

The saddest words in life are:
- It might have been...
- I should have...
- I could have...

- I wish I had...
- If only I had given a little extra...

When someone says, *I will do it one of these days*, you can be sure it means 'none of these days.'

A procrastinator's mindset goes, *I will leave home when all the traffic lights on my route turn green.* That will never happen!

Whatever dream God has put into your heart, it does not matter how hard it might be. Please do it now! Read and study Genesis 22:1.

Starting Early.

There is a saying that you do not need to rise early if you are strong. Some people are stronger, but can you imagine how much they would achieve if they started early? We must make ourselves do the things we have to do as early as possible. Whenever you begin your day on any project, you have an advantage over others by the time they wake up.

You Must be Willing to Start in a Small Way.

Big doors turn on small hinges. Most people want to begin not where they are but where they hope to be. Giant trees grow from tiny seeds. I do not know how old you are, but I can confidently say that you were not born at that age! Do not despise the day of small beginnings.

"Who (with reason) despises the day of small things? For

these seven shall rejoice when they see the plummet in the hand of Zerubbabel. (These seven) are the eyes of the lord which run to and fro throughout the whole earth." (Zechariah 4:10 Amplified Version)

Many have dreams in their hearts but die with them because they fear to start in a small way.

Jesus was born in a manger, but he conquered the whole world. My advice to you is, *Start now!*

A coach of a successful team was asked whether his team won because they had the will to win! He replied that, though it is essential to winning, what is more important is the will to start early and prepare to win. For Jesus to feed the multitudes, He needed only a few loaves of bread and a few fish.

"And He commanded the multitude to recline upon the ground, and He (then) took the seven loaves (of bread) and having given thanks, He needed them and kept on giving them to His disciples to put before (the people), and they placed them before the crowd." (Mark 8:6-8 Amplified Version)

Organize Your Life.

We must constantly improve in this area. When we fail in this area, we always make excuses as to why things are not working. The quality of your preparation will determine the quality of your performance. The organization is what you do before you do something. This means you must know what is more important in your life and work forward it daily.

Every dream has a starting, middle, and finishing phase. The way you handle the middle phase determines how you will finish. For most dreams, all we are required to do is have a proper foundation on which others will build even after we are gone to be with the Lord.

Many of us will never see the end of the dreams we started here on earth! Someone else will, but our responsibility is to lay a proper foundation for them. Will you make the sacrifice?

A Chinese saying goes: if you are planning for a year, grow rice. If you are planning for 20 years, grow trees. If you are planning for centuries, grow a man.

I will end by asking you this question! What is the number one thing you want to devote yourself to the rest of your life? If you had five minutes to live, what would you like to tell your family members and close friends? Would it be to show them your will?

Jesus Christ came to that moment in His life. He called those closest to him:

"Jesus approached and, breaking the silence, said to them, all authority (all power of rule) in heaven and on earth has been given to me. Go and make disciples of all the nations, baptizing them into the name of the Father and of the Son and of the Holy Spirit. Teaching them to observe everything that I have commanded you, and behold, I am with you all

the days (perpetually, uniformly, and on every occasion), to the (very) close and consumption of the age. Amen (so let it be)." (Matthew 28:18-20 Amplified Version)

That is God's dream and will for all those who love Him. Whatever your other dream may be, build it around this number one dream. It is a responsibility that has rewards in this life and in the life to come. It is a personal choice.

The greatest dream ever accomplished on earth was by Jesus Christ. He fought to the last drop of His blood but never gave up.

"Who for the joy that was set before Him endured the cross, despising the shame. And has sat down at the right hand of the throne of God." (Hebrews 12:2)

"Before He breathed his last, he declared "IT IS FINISHED" and bowing His head, He gave up His spirit." (John 19:30)

Before leaving this world, we must constantly seek His strength to finish whatever His dreams call us to. He has left us with the great commission to spread the good news of His mission, death, and resurrection.

You can participate in it by doing the following:

- Praying to the Lord of the harvest to send laborers. (Matthew 9:37-38)

- Going and telling the good news of Jesus Christ.

"But you shall receive power (ability, efficiency, and might) when the Holy Spirit has come upon you, and you shall be my witnesses in Jerusalem and all Judea and Samaria and to the ends (the very bounds) of the earth." (Acts 1:8 Amplified Version)

- Support those in the field with the resources God has placed within your reach.

Prayer of Agreement

"See I have this day set you over nations and the kingdoms, to root out, and to pull down, and to destroy and to overthrow, to build and to plant." (Jeremiah: 1:10)

Heavenly Father, I root out, pull down, destroy, and throw down every controlling force of Satan that has hindered the progress of the dreams of my friends who have read this book. I build and plant progress in all aspects of their dream today in the name of Jesus Christ our Lord.

Father, cause my friends to be fruitful and multiply and re-plenish the earth and subdue it through the dreams you have given them.

In the protecting power of Jesus, I cover their dreams with the blood of Jesus. I ask that you give them boldness, power, and faith to pursue these dreams. In the anointed name of Jesus Christ, I lift my friends and the dreams you have put in their hearts to you.

Anoint them and empower them over all principalities, powers, rulers of the darkness of this world, and every spiritual wickedness in high places. I confess victory, righteousness, protection, wealth, provision, and multiplication in every area of their lives in the glorious name of Jesus Christ, our Lord and Savior. AMEN.

Ministry Information

For more information regarding Go International Foundation and/or teaching materials, please feel free to contact us at:

Email: fredkasule@mail.com

www.gifuganda.org

Go International Foundation
P.O. Box 679
Kampala, Uganda, Africa

Other Books Written by Pastor Fred Kasule

Your Dream: The Power to Become

Grace for the Race

Built to Last

You Are God's Battle Axe

www.ingramcontent.com/pod-product-compliance
Lightning Source LLC
Chambersburg PA
CBHW071008120626
46546CB00003B/985